RENT
TO RENT 2.0

ISBN: 9798862443271
Imprint: Independently published

RENT
TO
RENT
2.0

The art of
cash flowing
a property you don't own.

SIMON SMITH

Acknowledgements

Mum and Dad, your son's a best selling author (let's put it out there). I'd like to take this opportunity to thank you for everything. Whilst always supporting my creative dreams, you encouraged me to get my foundations in place, a business management degree which I passed with first class honours. After over a decade of highs and lows in the music industry, I eventually needed to pivot, and being able to draw upon my education and business acumen was instrumental.

To my team. You make me look good. I can't tell you how much I appreciate your support, expertise and hard work. Trust me when I say, we're just getting started...

I'd like to thank all of the landlords and letting agents who unknowingly gave me the chance to do right by them and their properties. Over the past five years I'm proud to say that I have guaranteed over four million pounds of rent without fail (even through a pandemic).

Lastly, it wouldn't be right without me thanking my community; especially all of my mentees and masterminders who have implemented Rent-to-Rent 2.0. The results speak for themselves, and through your feedback I've been able to perfect these methods and put them down on paper.

Thanks

To Lucy,

My wife, soul mate and best friend.

Thank you for your unconditional support, always being ready to fight for us and inspiring me to make a change and create freedom in our lives.

None of this would be possible without you.

I guess Dorothy was right; "Simon is, not, to be underestimated." Neither are you.

P.S. Pebbles, I love you.

CONTENTS

Preface

The WHY?

Why do we do it? We spend our lives building someone else's dream, day after day, month after month, year after year. Until eventually we wake up grey and old, praying our pensions will be enough, hoping to have finally paid off our mortgage and then – and only then – can we truly start to enjoy some kind of freedom.

We prioritise deadlines, put up with our bosses and miss out on lost time doing what we love with the people we care for most. And worst of all, we do it all knowingly for a measly carrot they slyly dangle in front of us which pays us just enough to sell our souls every morning, but never enough for us to buy our freedom back. It's a trap and very few ever escape.

The system is broken (at least for us it is). Why wait 25 years to start living? I want to live today.

Monopoly is a lot like real life for people wanting to build wealth with property. Buy up as much as you can and you will earn effortlessly in your sleep from tenants that will pay you every time they land on your house. The issue is the game – in real life that is – isn't accessible for people like you and me to win. And we naively are the losers that keep rolling the dice and taking chances, praying that we will make ends meet.

The reality is harsh: it's only a matter of time before we have to pay the winners and the banker, and for many of us that means never saving enough capital to invest in property ourselves; and as a result we end up trapped in the rat race.

This book is your ticket to change that. It changes all the traditional property investment rules and gives you the opportunity of earning without owning. Simply put, you can control all the property you could ever wish for without needing the capital to buy it. The results are staggering.

First, you start building your own cash flow from property, then you can replace your income. Next, you can take care of friends and family, and remove yourself from the business to free up your time and take complete control of your life today, not in 25 years. But there's more, once you've put your seatbelt on and you make the rules to your life, you can then reinvest that income into property that you do own for long-term legacy wealth.

Over the past five years I've done just that. I've controlled over 60 properties and generated multi-million pounds of rental income from property I don't own, and reinvested in property I do own so my wife and I will never have to work again. This book is about me sharing this with you. No sales. No pitching. Just a detailed account of everything I have learnt to help you build wealth with property, without ever owning it.

If it can help just one of you escape the rat race then it was all worthwhile.

Enjoy.
Simon

Introduction

There I was, sat on the edge of my seat, hooked by the vision of how my life "could be". Quitting the grind of the 9–5 and replacing my income with steady, predictable cash flow... it was the dream we all wanted. I was sitting in yet another "free" property course with at least 200 other aspiring property investors, as we all listened intently and braced ourselves. We were about to find out how to unlock the secret of property investment and how to become "financially free"!

Why was I sitting there, wide-eyed and practically drooling over the promises of yet another "property guru"? To the outside world, it might have seemed that I'd had a successful decade in the music industry, touring the world and writing songs for stars. In reality, I was over 30 years old and I had no savings, no solid reliable income and no pension. What I did have was a pile of student loan debt and self-assessment tax bills I couldn't afford to pay off.

On top of this my wedding to the love of my life, Lucy, was coming up fast. I was painfully conscious that we didn't even have a place we could call our own to live in – I had rented my entire life. A few weeks previously, I had decided enough was enough. I needed to make change happen – and fast.

After exploring every business I could think of, as well as the stock market and crypto trading, I eventually gave up and decided I had no choice but to find myself a "proper stable job". What the Indeed listing had sworn would be an interview for a decent sales role with a Nottingham-based agency ended up being a humiliating experience. I found myself in a "group interview" with 20 to 30 other poor souls trying to sell home insurance to random passers-by on a freezing street outside a Co-op.

I had thought that trying to make a living off irregular and unreliable royalty checks from songwriting was bad... this was worse. After I had snuck away and into the disabled toilet of the Costa Coffee across the street, I stared hard at myself in the mirror and wondered "what am I doing?" I had officially hit rock bottom.

I frantically searched the pockets of my cheap baggy suit for my phone. I had to call Lucy. She was at work, she shouldn't have answered her phone – what could she have done anyway? But, she must have realised it was important from the persistence of the ring tone.

After I unloaded the events of the morning on her, the line went quiet. Her answer was just two words, but I'll never forget them: "Come home."

Tony Robbins famously said "change only comes when the pain of staying the same is greater than the pain of change." At that point, the pain had become real. Change was coming and I was finally ready for it.

And so, like so many desperate people before me, I found myself on a free property course, swearing to myself that this was simply market research and I would absolutely not be signing up for any paid courses. No way.

So when I was offered a course on something called "deal sourcing" that claimed to be worth £15,000, for just £1,997 (a limited-time offer, of course), I obviously almost ran to throw myself into the jaws of the vultures at the back of the room with card machines ready to extract my life savings and send me further into debt.

For many of you, this may be a familiar experience.

Halfway to the open arms of the sales team, I thought of Lucy and our upcoming wedding – she needed a say in this. She accepted another phone call out of the blue – this time full of excitement. When asked if it was OK to use the card we'd been planning to fund the wedding catering with, her response was "if it feels right, do it".

So I did. No turning back now.

The course was fascinating, I soaked up every detail the expert speakers had to share. The issue was that I kept feeling that certain bits of key information were missing. When it turned out that this information and the all-important on-going support and mentorship I'd need would come at a further cost of £10,000, I decided I was out. I went home, put on a brave face (at least tried to) and went at it alone.

I was out of my comfort zone, learning a lot and building relationships with local agents... but it wasn't quite right. I needed a reliable and consistent monthly income and deal sourcing was just too hit-and-miss. It had all the same issues I had been facing with music's unreliable royalty checks: every first of the month I was back to zero with a mountain to climb.

It was time for something drastic. By exhausting all the resources available to me – selling my dream car and borrowing from my parents – I scraped together the money I needed to buy a property for myself, instead of brokering it for someone else.

After putting it all on the line and using every penny to my name for the deposit and refurb (about £30,000), I was able to get tenants in and start making a clean £600 in cash flow. But, £600 a month wasn't enough to live off, not even close – I needed to scale and get more property, but there was one problem. Where on earth was I going to find the money for another deposit?

I needed a strategy that'd give me consistent and fast cash flow, without requiring too much capital upfront. I also needed it to be something I could scale to buy more property. After hours of researching and reflecting on the options, I realised there was only really one choice: rent-to-rent.

In other words, rather than having to find a deposit to purchase my next buy-to-let property, I would simply find a motivated landlord that would allow me to guarantee their rent for five years. I would do some light cosmetic improvements, furnish the place and then rent it out on a room-by-room or nightly basis for a premium.

Anything after the landlord's monthly rent and my expenses would be mine to keep: if done correctly, the monthly cash flow would be the same as a traditional property investment (if not more). Genius.

With just £3,000 left to my name, I quickly got set-up, compliant and hunting for my first deal. It was tough, with constant no's and setbacks, but I eventually found the perfect deal – the landlord would hand over their property to me, let me do all the heavy lifting and in return I would get to keep the net cash flow.

My £3,000 wasn't enough for what I needed, so I had to borrow another £4,000. A small price compared to the chunky deposit required to buy a place. Just two weeks later I had fully tenanted the property and started making over £800 net cash flow per month.

My approach was rough around the edges, but I had the basic formula.

Over the next five years I would develop this strategy into a reliable, step-by-step framework which has provided me with the security I had been looking for ever since I left the music business. I call it Rent-to-Rent 2.0. With it, I have built a 7-figure Rent-to-Rent 2.0 business that has completely transformed my life. At the time of writing this book, I manage over 50 properties and have used the cash flow to build a seven-figure portfolio of property I have purchased for myself.

The best part is that as I've fine-tuned the strategy, I've passed on my knowledge and helped hundreds of people get started and become financially independent through my unique strategy; Rent-to-Rent 2.0.

It wasn't all easy though. The thing is, when I was starting out, I had no clue what I was doing. So much of the content out there for rent-to-rent is either looking at things through rose-tinted glasses or trying to monetise you and sell courses. Nobody is taking rent-to-rent as a serious career in property and so many rookies are doing it poorly.

There needs to be a better way. Rent-to-rent has the potential to change your life, but there needs to be a focus on educating people about how to do things right without having to mess up first.

This book is here to change that. It's a record of what I have learnt through hard work, making my many mistakes along the way and pushing uphill with every step.

What *is* Rent-to-Rent?

Now, I know what you're probably thinking here. "Why would a landlord give you their property and allow you to make all the money? Isn't that illegal subletting?!"

I get it – if it sounds too good to be true usually it is, right! I know, I thought that too. But here is the thing… When you think about it, every landlord wants the same thing: rent every month, minimal headaches and a tenant that will take good care of their property. So when you understand that rent-to-rent does all that (and more) for the landlord, suddenly it starts to make sense.

Imagine you were a landlord, what would you say if someone offered you a guaranteed rent payment every month for five years, handled the tenants and managed all the maintenance, so that you could sit back and relax. You'd jump on it, right? So, the next question is why would someone bother to do that? It seems like a lot of hard work. What happens if you can't guarantee the rent? Sounds like a big risk!

Well, when done properly – after conducting the right due diligence and using the correct paperwork – you can get a huge return on your investment. In my opinion, the greatest. If you put in a seven grand investment, you can make it back within six months if you do it right. After those six months, the other four and a half *years* would just be pure profit!

The more I dug into it, the more I realised how crazy the cash flow from it could be. Depending on the property and your preference, you could rent out a property on a long-term basis room-by-room or you could rent it out nightly as a serviced accommodation.

On top of this, you don't have to worry about the costs you normally get in property. There is no mortgage, no deposits, no stamp duty and no waiting for months for the deal to close.

Sure, it wasn't entirely free to set up – you need to make an initial investment to refurb the place and to refurb and furnish the property – but compared

Introduction

to buy-to-let, the outlay is minimal! A buy-to-let takes years to pay off the initial investment. Rent-to-rent would take just months *and* I could have the keys within just days of finding the deal!

JOHN AND MIKE
Rent-to-Rent vs buy-to-let

Let me paint you a picture of how much easier rent-to-rent can be to get started and how amazing the return on investment is.

John and Mike are mates who are both looking for their first investment property. Interestingly, they manage to find two brilliant properties that are almost identical and worth £200,000 each.

Now, John doesn't know what he doesn't know, but he is adamant that he wants a "solid and safe" investment property that he "owns". So, when Mike (who has been doing his research) tells him it'd probably be better to rent-to-rent them – they would get essentially all the benefits for a fraction of the investment – John can't believe it.

They decide to have a bet about who can get the best returns. John will buy his property and let it out, while Mike will convince the landlord to rent to him so he can run it as rent-to-rent. After a year, they would compare and see who was doing better.

To get his property, John puts down a 25 per cent deposit of £50,000. On top of this, he needs to fork out £6000 in stamp duty and £2000 in legal fees. Once he has furnished and refurbished for £5000, John has invested £63,000 in his property.

Mike, on the other hand, isn't buying the property so he doesn't need to pay nearly as much. He just needs to spend £1,300 on legal fees and another £5,000 to furnish the place. In total, he just needs to invest only £6,300 compared to John's £63,000.

Once they've filled their properties, they both start getting the same rental income – £2,400 a month. John is delighted, all he needs to worry about is paying a few hundred in bills and mortgage payments – everything else, he gets to keep as his monthly cash flow, a tidy £1,250 net sum. Mike has no mortgage, but has to pay the guaranteed rent to the landlord in addition to the bills! Over half of what he makes disappears, ending up with a monthly cash flow of £1,000 – less than John.

At the end of the year, however, Mike is the one who's laughing. He broke even after just six months and has made £5,700 in profit already, with a massive 90 per cent return on investment! John however is still paying off his initial investment. He's still got three years and a bit before he's making money. While John's waiting for the value of his property to increase, Mike could be

17

doing ten rent-to-rents a year – making a staggering return on investment of over ten times!

The more I looked into rent-to-rent, the more I started wondering why more people weren't talking about it. It's not a particularly complicated concept after all. It happens all the time in the property industry.

It's simply a way of controlling a property without owning it yourself – like leasing it. The commercial world has been doing this for years. A company will lease a building and then use it as a hotel. A shopping centre will lease out units for businesses to use as shops. If you can lease a building and operate a commercial business from it, why not provide accommodation?

The advantages of rent-to-rent

The power of rent-to-rent is that it is a scalable business. With the amount of money it takes to buy a property, I could rent perhaps ten. Once each is up and running, I can start making a profit in under a year, rather than waiting for my buy-to-let to just break even. After I am making money, then I can just reinvest back into the business and keep scaling.

Another benefit is that it is recession-proof – particularly compared to buy-to-let. Since you don't have a mortgage to pay off, you are insulated from high interest rates. With buy-to-let, you might find your profits dropping from a grand to just £400. In rent-to-rent, your rent is locked in and your profits won't be touched – boom!

On top of that, quality accommodation is always in demand which helps protect you from other issues. During Covid-19 other businesses really suffered. I remember that at one point after Boris told everyone to lockdown, Airbnb just... closed. I ended up spending several sleepless nights trying desperately to work out how I'd pay the £20,000 of rent per month I was guaranteeing at the time.

In the end things were only bad for a few weeks, then the market came back stronger than ever. Other forms of demand for accommodation took over. I ended up renting to construction workers, hospital staff and people shielding or isolating themselves away from vulnerable family members.

Introduction

As I had realised back when I started looking at property – everyone is always going to want a quality place to stay or live.

When things aren't doing so well is when the final overlooked advantage of rent-to-rent comes in. While many might see it as more risky than buy-to-let, realistically it is far easier to exit or pull out of a property when things are going bad, if needed. If you had bought the property, then you would need to go through the long and expensive hassle of selling it. If you are just renting, all you need to do is give two months notice and then hand the keys back when it doesn't work.

Sure, the ultimate aim is to build assets that you *do* own, but here's the thing. If you invest all your capital into one property just to brag down the pub that you "own it," you will run out of money and be stuck like me after my first property purchase. On the other hand, if you see rent-to-rent as leverage, you can create massive cash flow and then use that income to fund your freedom and later buy properties. This way, you will never run out of funds and your initial capital will compound fast!

What you will learn in this book

Rent-to-rent genuinely changed my life. It let me go from spending every minute I wasn't working worrying about money, to actually reclaiming control of my life and time.

These days, I have built myself a reputation, first as one of the biggest rent-to-rent businesses in the UK, and now I have also established myself as a leading property investment coach. Nobody else online offers as much specialist rent-to-rent content as I do. However, I have had to work for every lesson learnt and experience gained. You shouldn't have to wing it and work things out the hard way.

This is the book that I wish I had had when I started out and explains the better way to operate rent-to-rent that I had to work out for myself – Rent-to-Rent 2.0.

Part 1 guides you through the process of getting set up for Rent-to-Rent 2.0. There is so much that can be done before you even step foot in a property. If you do this right, this means that your life will be just so much easier and you'll save yourself time and the headaches of making your own mistakes when you could just learn from mine.

Part 2 talks about a particularly important challenge. How do I find people to rent from and how do I get them interested in signing an agreement? There is an art to this, I want to share a framework that allows you to uncover their key motivators and add value they had only dreamt of. Do this right and you'll build your own waiting list of prospects lining up to work with you, time and time again.

Part 3 is all about cash flowing your deals to create the all-important income that you are aiming for. Having a structured and deliberate approach allows you to get things done right the first time. This means that you can start getting a reliable cash flow quickly and painlessly without having to guess and potentially slip up along the way.

There is a better way to be successful in rent-to-rent. Are you ready to get started?

CHAPTER 1

Rent–to–Rent 2.0 – A better way to earn from property

There are a lot of rogue rent-to-renters out there fresh from free property courses or having watched a YouTube video or two. They then mindlessly go around offering landlords a guaranteed rent with no true knowledge, experience, or capital to back up their promises.

These rent-to-renters are completely unprepared. They are largely under-educated and nobody has told them how to get themselves correctly set up. This means that they have no credibility, experience and in many cases have not acquired the correct compliance to legally operate as a rent-to-renter. Not a good start.

When they approach a landlord or letting agent, it's obvious they have no clue what they are talking about and so, guess what, no deals. They are wandering around offering something huge – guaranteeing somebody's rent – with absolutely no reason to take them seriously. They automatically have the weaker hand because they look desperate, trying to control property they can't afford. They are trying to be A-players in an industry they don't understand.

The problem isn't really with rent-to-rent itself. The problem is how they are positioning themselves. The property industry has some deeply-ingrained misconceptions and opinions on rent-to-rent and how credible it is. It's time we changed the narrative.

Misconceptions and biases around rent-to-rent

Fundamentally, property tends to be a bit conservative and resistant to new ideas. Your average landlord is likely to be someone from an older generation who's already made their money and has been doing things the same way for years. Even when they're not, it's hard to escape the traditional "right" way of doing things.

The real reason why landlords and agents often don't want to give rent-to-rent the time of day is just because they're not used to it. You can also come across a lot of prejudice towards rent-to-rent as a business, mostly due to biases and beliefs about what property *should* be.

It's time for a fresher approach to property – it's time to break free from those old-fashioned views and embrace rent-to-rent for what it can offer. Some of the main myths I've encountered around rent-to-rent are:

It only counts if you own it

Way back when, ownership was a big deal. It didn't matter if it was property, cars, or your mobile phone – if you didn't outright own it, it was worth less. What the traditionalists in property aren't realising is that we aren't in an ownership economy anymore.

Look at some of the best business models in any industry right now. Very few of them actively *own* what they are selling you. Uber doesn't own the cars. Airbnb doesn't own the property. Amazon doesn't own the brands or products they sell. What they have is control.

These days, you can lease pretty much anything you want. As a result, you get more flexibility and when times get hard, you have less stuff weighing you down to lose. In a world where interest rates and bills are going through the roof, the fact that you don't own the property yourself, yet you receive all the benefits of doing so, is powerful.

The more it costs you, the better it is

Educators selling traditional rent-to-rent often present it as a "no money down" property strategy. This means that people can get snobbish about it, dismissing it as a poor man's strategy that shouldn't be taken seriously.

Rent-to-rent isn't really "no money down". However, it's certainly one of the cheapest ways to get started in property, but it does take money to make sure the property is worth renting. I recommend at least seven grand as a rule of thumb – I'll talk about this more in Chapter 2.

But remember, the real power of rent-to-rent is that the economies of scale are remarkable. It's true you could get one deal for a few grand. You could also make a huge profit by investing 60 grand and getting 10 deals that could generate you a six-figure salary!

You have to be desperate to do it

Since so many rent-to-renters are just winging it, they have trouble attracting the landlords with really high quality properties. This means they have to lower their standards and start attracting a terrible quality of landlord and property.

This ends up becoming a self-perpetuating problem. Since none of the more desirable landlords will give you the time of day, you're stuck with the lower quality properties. Guess what? Lower quality houses means the amount you can charge tenants or guests is also lower. As a result, your cash flow is reduced – making it hard for you to move up the ladder.

Of course, if you weren't desperate before you worked with a bad landlord – you will be afterwards, trust me!

Working with a landlord who doesn't see the value in the service we offer will never end well. While some newbies often put landlords on a pedestal, taking on anyone that is open to the arrangement, not all landlords are equal. We must approach with caution – any good rent-to-rent deal is 50 per cent the property and 50 per cent the landlord.

I've learned to choose carefully – if you don't, you will be taken advantage of. You might be expected to fund maintenance that's out of your control or be blamed for damp, mould and broken fixtures that had been there since before you arrived. After surviving this for months to years, you might then have the rent hiked up mid-term with little to no appreciation for the guaranteed rent you have delivered so far.

Rent-to-rent can absolutely offer something that any landlord would benefit from. Search for the landlords that will appreciate you, give you the freedom to do business without too much interference and will cooperate with you when things need doing to the property. Landlords like this will understand the value in having a professional look after their assets. The trick is demonstrating to these savvy people that you can provide something valuable to them. That you are a *professional*.

At the end of the day, these beliefs aren't true. The problem is that the way rent-to-rent is presented and sold works against it. A traditional rent-to-rent approach does very little to change these prejudices. Before we can really get started, we need to change how we position it.

This sounds a lot like subletting. Subletting is illegal, right?
Most standard Assured Shorthand Tenancy Agreements (ASTs) do prohibit subletting. If a tenant is approved to enter into a tenancy agreement with a landlord and then goes behind their back to sublet the property to someone else, it's clear to see that this would breach the terms of the AST and cause serious issues.

However, if you have the landlord's consent, are fully compliant and use the correct agreements, then rent-to-rent is perfectly legal. The problem is a lot of uneducated rent-to-renters may not know this and, therefore, unintentionally operate illegally.

Rent-to-Rent 2.0 –
A more professional approach

The main difference with Rent-to-Rent 2.0 is that we actually deliver the value in our offer. We don't present ourselves as desperate property investors who can't afford our own properties. Instead, we position ourselves as expert professionals offering a premium service.

This starts by adopting this professional and prepared mindset, and then backing it up with hard proof that you can put your money where your mouth is. By reading this book, you'll learn how to get the results that prove you are a credible professional. With this, you will quickly discover that you now have the upper hand. The savvy landlords of higher quality properties will start coming to you.

Once you're established, you can then fully systemise the business and build a team to operate the business for you while you sit back and enjoy the returns!

Professional presentation
The first and most important part of Rent-to-Rent 2.0 is presenting yourself as a professional. This means that you need to be prepared, educated and that you have set yourself up properly.

Instead of winging it like a newbie rent-to-renter, you need to be able to position yourself as somebody who knows what they are doing and what they are talking about. To do this, you need to educate yourself. A confident and professional mindset is much easier when you realise you know more than most landlords and letting agents!

Reading this book is the all-important first step. By following my advice, you can learn what you need to know to get set up and close your deals with confidence.

A scalable business model

One of the biggest differences between Rent-to-Rent 2.0 and traditional approaches is how it looks at cash flow and scaling as a business.

Traditional rent-to-rent tends to view doing deals as a means to an end. The goal is to go in, make money quickly on a short-term basis, then move onto something more "serious". Is it any wonder landlords don't take it as seriously?

It makes me laugh when people are surprised that I'm still actively running my rent-to-rent business long after being financially independent from properties I "own". But the fact is, rent-to-rent still provides the best return of all of my property investments – so why on earth would I stop doing it?

Rent-to-Rent 2.0 is a legitimate business in its own right, not just a stepping stone towards some other goal. Its aim is to generate the cash flow with which you can scale the business over time and build it into a sustainable long-term venture. This happens over four steps:

- Build your initial investment: Starting in rent-to-rent is not free – no matter what some might say. You need to have money to get started and cover any initial rent payments, or fees, and to do your first cosmetic refurb.
- Get cash flow: Once you have your first deal set up and you are receiving rent from the tenants or guests, you start getting cash flow. This is the difference between the total money you make and any costs you have to pay (or recoup).
- Reinvest your cash flow: Once you have started getting cash flow, you can reinvest that money into your next deals. This ends up turning into a cycle where you can continue to scale and grow as a business organically.
- Diversify: Eventually, it becomes a good idea to diversify so that you are not just relying on one stream of income. You might start by operating rent-to-rent at first, then move into using the properties you decide not to acquire to source deals for others. Eventually, you reinvest money into assets you own for long-term, bulletproof, legacy wealth.

Flexibility of approach

Generally, there are two approaches to running traditional rent-to-rent:

- A house in multiple occupation (HMO) in which you rent the entire property from the landlord for a fixed monthly guaranteed rent, carry out a light cosmetic refurb, and fully furnish the property. You then rent the rooms out on an individual basis for a premium and pay the bills. What's left is your profit (aka cash flow).
- Serviced accommodation (SA), which is where you add value and offer the property fully-serviced on a nightly basis.

HMOs explained

An HMO is also sometimes called a houseshare. Basically, it is a property rented by at least three people who aren't from the same 'household' (the same family for example), but share facilities like the bathroom and kitchen.

If you are renting out a property as an HMO in England or Wales, you might be required to have a licence to do so depending on the area. If you are renting out a large HMO, you must have a licence. A property is defined as a large HMO if all of the following apply:

- It is rented to five or more people who form more than one household
- Some or all tenants share toilet, bathroom or kitchen facilities
- At least one tenant pays rent (or their employer pays it for them)

Even if your property is smaller and rented to fewer people, you may still need a licence. You may also be required to obtain planning permission when converting a single home or residential property (C3 use class) into a HMO (C4 use class) if you are investing in an Article 4 area. Check with your council.[1]

HMO's have become increasingly popular for their convenience to both professional and student tenants who can walk into a fully furnished property, pay a fixed monthly rent usually all-inclusive of bills, and co-live with other like minded people! Dividing a house into individual rooms allows rent-to-renters to increase the total achievable rent for a property substantially meaning that they can pay the landlord a fair rent, cover the bills and still make a nice cash flow for themselves. Genius.

---

1   House in multiple occupation licence. (n.d.). GOV.UK. Retrieved August 8, 2023, from https://www.gov.uk/find-licences/house-in-multiple-occupation-licence.

What is SA?

An SA is when a property is fully furnished and rented to "guests", not tenants, with hotel-like services. SA properties should have everything the client may need for their stay, which can vary in lengths from a one night stay to guests needing temporary accommodation for longer durations.

With the rise of Online Travel Agents such as Airbnb, SA has boomed and more and more people are choosing to stay in self-contained properties rather than more traditional hotels. Advantages include your own lounge, a kitchen for you to store and prepare your own meals and the privacy to settle in and make it a home away from home. SA is another amazing way for rent-to-renters to maximise the income from a property and in doing so allow for a profit to be made.

Whilst, unlike HMO, no licences are currently required, there is still some legislation in certain areas that need to be adhered to such as London's 90-day rule.[2]

Most traditional rent-to-rent experts will tell you to pick one or the other and stick with it. What I quickly realised was that a hybrid approach was possible. Instead of limiting yourself to just one, you use whichever fits a specific property best. Not only is this smart in terms of diversification, but it gives you the best of both worlds: recurring reliable income (HMO) and big chunks of cash (SA) – the perfect cocktail.

A valuable solution

The reason that this works is rent-to-rent absolutely solves a very real problem.

In property management, there are loads of scary, tough things that might put people off actually getting into property. This might include dealing with nightmare tenants, keeping up with any new regulations the government or local councils might impose, or just the day-to-day stress of always being on call for maintenance or whatever minor issue a tenant might have.

If you are a professional landlord, you signed up for that – you might even have a dedicated management team to handle it. Professional landlords know

---

2   For more information on this please visit: https://www.gov.uk/government/speeches/short-term-use-of-residential-property-in-london

what they are doing to get the highest possible returns. The thing is, not many landlords are professional landlords.

Even particularly savvy landlords might not have the time, energy, or know-how to stay on top of their property (or properties) without it becoming a full-time job they really don't want. The thought of hassle and headaches like constant tenant turnover, nightmare tenants that can't be evicted, or never-ending property maintenance fills them with dread.

In most cases though, you're not offering a service for the professional landlords – they've got it covered already. Though once you master this, they will come to you too as they begin to wind down for retirement and become tired of the workload and attention required. The landlords who will be queuing up for your help are the ones who are feeling desperate and overwhelmed or are increasingly realising that their time is their most valuable asset.

All these landlords need is somebody reliable to manage their property for them and provide them with that elusive passive income they all want, but until now have struggled to achieve.

Enter you. The Rent-to-Rent 2.0 investor with the answer to all their problems. Though hopefully lacking the poorly-fitting suit and shoe combo...

Three Landlord profiles you need to know about

It is possible to sort the landlords who benefit from your services into several general categories, including:

1. Accidental landlords
2. Motivated landlords
3. Sophisticated landlords

Accidental landlords are landlords who have ended up in charge of managing a property they either can't look after themselves or need help with. How they end up in this situation can vary, such as:

1. Inheriting a property they don't know what to do with
2. Needing to relocate urgently for work and they either can't or don't want to sell their original property
3. Becoming unable to manage the property themselves, either due to age or health issues

What an accidental landlord wants from you is someone who can help make managing their property less overwhelming for them.

Introduction

Motivated landlords have been burnt in the past – either by bad tenants or poor letting agents. What these bad experiences might look like is different from case to case, including:

1. Non-paying tenants
2. Tenants trashing their property
3. Letting agents who neglected their responsibilities to maintain the property – while charging extortionate commissions and maintenance fees

A motivated landlord simply wants to be able to trust that their property is in good hands and that they won't be burnt again.

Sophisticated landlords value their time and resources. They want their property to be well-managed and maintained, since that is how they maximise their returns. However, they would prefer to reclaim their time and have someone else ensure that their property is looked after for them.

Now, it's true that letting agents will often offer a service which will manage a property for the landlord. But, this isn't always exactly what the landlord wants. It is sad, but the harsh truth is that many agents offering a management service often don't care about the property beyond earning their commission.

In the end, a letting agent is going to be managing so many properties at once, it is hard to give it the full care and attention that a landlord deserves. This of course can be an opportunity for you – it is possible to do deals with letting agents that let you take on many properties in one go. We'll talk more about this later!

A letting agent's services also don't typically add value to the property, meaning that the property will become more and more tired and run-down over time. In rent-to-rent we offer support in refurbishing and maintaining the property as part of our services. Our goal isn't just to keep the property in one piece, we want to be renting out quality accommodation. This means that it's in our best interest to get stuck in and make sure that everything stays in tip-top condition.

This can be a huge incentive for any landlord, but particularly an accidental landlord. Since they fell into the property game without ever really intending to, investing in the property can sometimes be hard. They might not have the experience or awareness of how much value they get from investing in their property. It might also be that they simply don't have the capital to do it – they didn't plan or budget to be investing in a property that they didn't even intend to be renting out in the first place.

Then we come along, offer to freshen things up a bit and make their life easy! They basically get their asset improved without them having to really lift a finger. Even if they don't get why it is important, it's hard to argue with the results when it's staring them in the face!

With us in their corner, a landlord doesn't need to worry about all the work and effort it takes to be a professional landlord. Our role as a professional rent to-rent organisation is to be the professional landlord for them, while they spend their time and energy on what they would rather be doing.

In short, rent-to-rent really deserves a far better reputation than it has in the property business right now. The thing is, with how some people operate, you can't always blame people for not trusting it. It's easy to be sceptical if you only ever hear about unprofessional people and negative experiences.

Rent-to-Rent 2.0 is the answer. If the only reason people aren't convinced by rent-to-rent is because cowboys aren't approaching it properly, the trick is to be the professional who knows what you are doing. So, instead of charging right into the viewings, let's start at the beginning with getting the planning and preparation done right.

PART ONE

Get prepared with a professional set-up

Part one: Get prepared with a professional set-up

Rent-to-rent is a fantastic opportunity to earn a tidy income through a business which is stable and scalable. When it starts working, the sky is the limit! The key to making it work is to get started in a sensible and structured way. No blagging it. If you want to work with decent landlords who won't mess you around, you need to give them a reason to trust that you know what you are doing.

With Rent-to-Rent 2.0, that's a straightforward job! What will make a landlord value your offer is being able to position yourself as an expert who is offering a premium service that serves the landlord's needs. Before you worry about viewings or talking to landlords, you need to do some legwork in order to help you create that professional foundation.

Chapter 2 talks about the first step – giving yourself a reality check about what you want to achieve and why you want to do it. Having clear and achievable goals means it is far easier to get things done, rather than randomly doing whatever and praying that it works.

It is also a good time to start thinking about what you have and what you need – whether it is time, money, skills, or people. Trust me, it can get embarrassing if it's clear you are out of your depth when it matters most. Starting to build strategies to make sure you are prepared when you need it allows you to know what you're on about when it counts.

Next, you need to start establishing the credibility that means that landlords and agents won't just laugh in your face when you pitch your services. Landlords will have certain expectations of what a professional operation looks like. The more you can do to start meeting those expectations from day one, the easier it will be to position yourself as someone they can trust to manage their property and guarantee their rent.

Chapter 3 explains how through setting up a business and building up your brand, you have something concrete to show a landlord, or agent, that showcases your offer and builds credibility.

Chapter 4 shows you how to find the perfect investment area and how to conduct the necessary market research. If you want to generate a stable cash flow from a property, you need to have a solid idea of what you actually want to do with it. You can't do that without understanding your area first.

Getting market research right makes the whole process of rent-to-rent easier. It allows you to know which areas are going to be more valuable to you and start building a profile of the tenants or guests you want to attract. Most importantly, it means you can work out if the place is a deal and that you are going to get a return on your investment before committing to guaranteeing the rent for five years.

This is essential for negotiation. Nothing says that you're a pro quite like being able to back yourself up with the numbers immediately when trying to get the deal over the line. It also saves you running around after a property that isn't worth your time.

Like with any investment, there is an element of risk. I've seen so many people lose money and I don't want you to be one of them. In this section, I will outline how to make sure that doesn't happen to you by getting the set-up right from the start.

CHAPTER 2

What do you *really* want?

Rent-to-Rent 2.0 is not going to be for everyone. While it can offer amazing rewards when it works, it is not going to be some get-rich-quick scheme. It requires you to invest time, money and effort for it to be worth it.

It is simple. Not easy.

If you want things to work out, you can't just chance it and hope. You need to have a strategy to help you work out what you're doing and why. This comes in three steps:

1. Being clear and honest with yourself about WHY you have chosen to do rent-to-rent
2. Setting specific goals so you know what success will look like
3. Assessing your resources to work out if you have what you need to get started – and how to make up for what you're missing

What motivates you?

The first question is why you actually want to get into property. It is really important to be as honest and specific about this with yourself as possible. This is the fundamental driving force behind why you are doing this. It is what you will need to tap into to stay motivated when things get tough – and they will.

Don't confuse this with your objectives. It is easy to go "I want to have ten properties" – that's your property goal. "I want to have a lot of properties so I can make loads of money" isn't quite right either – that's your financial goal, though a pretty terrible one because you haven't made it specific. These are important, but superficial. They come later.

At this point we are looking for the deep truth: what does success in property and rent-to-rent actually *do* in your life? A deeper motivation might sound more like this:

"I'm uncertain about my job – I've heard rumours that I may be getting made redundant. My wife is a stay-at-home mum to our three kids and, therefore, the sole responsibility of keeping a roof over our head is on me. We have limited savings and so we could be in deep trouble if I lose my job. I need to take matters into my own hands and create a new income stream."

For me, my motivation always was that I was afraid of my future. I had no assets, no pension, no stable income, and no solid plans to change it. I was sick of being helpless and reliant on external factors for income and needed a stable source of income so that I could be self-sufficient and provide for my family.

Being able to remind yourself of your motivation isn't meant to tell you *what* you are doing, but *why.* There were so many times that being able to look at mine helped me keep going when things got rough.

Setting your specific goals

Once you know why you are getting into rent-to-rent, it's time for you to start setting yourself specific goals or objectives you want to achieve.

On a general level, the point of these goals is to satisfy your fundamental motivations. It's at this point that you can consider turning a "why" like "we are losing our main income if I get made redundant." into "what do I need to do to make X amount of money in Y amount of time."

When talking about specific goals, I divide them into three categories:

- Property goals – How many properties you expect to be managing – do you want just a handful, or are you aiming to become a property mogul?
- Financial goals – How much income do you need to get from rent-to-rent in order to satisfy your motivation?
- Time management goals – How are you intending to use your time and how much of your week are you intending to spend on your rent-to-rent business?

Property goals – How many is actually enough?

Of these, the property goals aren't actually the priority right now. I see so many beginner rent-to-renters setting themselves property goals – telling themselves they need to have 15 properties by the end of the year – but they're failing to see the big picture.

Take it from me, less is more here. You don't want more properties just for the sake of it. More properties means more work. You have more houses to fill and manage, and more tenants or landlords to deal with. It can quickly become a headache, particularly when you're just starting out.

Nine times out of ten, what you really want isn't more properties. When you set an ambitious property goal, what you actually want is more cash flow. If you can get the cash flow to meet your financial goals from two properties rather than four, that is a far better deal. One high quality property is always going to be worth more than several below-average ones.

Imagine – your financial goal is to generate £3,000 per month in the next three months. If each property generates an average of £1,000 per month, then you would need three properties. However, if you had two properties that generated £1,500 per month, you're getting the same result for just two thirds of the time and energy. Quality beats quantity every time.

This is something I learnt the hard way. When I got started, my big "why" was that I was at rock bottom and couldn't see any other way forward. If I didn't do something, I was scared that I could find myself selling home insurance outside of a Co-op in the rain for the rest of my life.

My first goal was realistic – I just wanted to have one property. After I got that, I went a little overboard. I set myself the huge goal of getting 20 properties within just one year, and I did just that. But, then I realised with a lot of properties came a lot of responsibility which I wasn't prepared for and I didn't have the systems in place yet.

My priority was the number of properties, so I had ended up acquiring properties just for the sake of getting one step closer to my goal. A year or so later, this became problematic since I didn't have the time or expertise to manage everything by myself. My advice is to set realistic property goals. As you go along, then you learn the process and set up the infrastructure so that you are fully prepared to scale your Rent-to-Rent 2.0 business.

Financial goals –
Getting the cash flow you need

The most common financial goal I come across is "I want to replace my income." The reasons might be different – you're sick of your job, you hate your boss, you want to spend more time with your family – but the end result is you still need to make a living.

Regardless of whether you are trying to replace your work income, pay off a mortgage, prepare for retirement, not go back to work after maternity leave or even put your kids through university, you need to have a number you are aiming for.

Not only will it set a clear roadmap for hitting that goal – making it more attainable – but it lets you easily see the point at which you're generating "extra" cash flow. Anything you make beyond your base line can be reinvested to scale the business and ultimately hire someone else to do the heavy lifting for you!

Something to remember with Rent-to-Rent 2.0 is that there are two phases to it. The first is creating cash flow from property you don't own. The second is to ultimately start reinvesting into properties that you do own.

Having a steady cash flow is what allows rent-to-rent to scale. Once you are getting a consistent income from one property, you can then redirect any profits into setting up the next deal. However, keep in mind that these deals aren't going to last forever. While some landlords might decide to renew, others will take their property back at the end of the term and that cash flow will be gone.

Once your financial goals are being met, in order to guarantee long-term legacy wealth, you purchase assets that are equal to your cash flow goal. At this point, you've made it! You now have a choice: stop and consolidate or scale.

Time management goals –
How are you spending your time?

If the financial side of rent-to-rent is about having a consistent income, the time side of things is not much different. Rent-to-rent takes persistence to pay off.

I see some rent-to-renters booking five days off their demanding jobs to devote every hour to chasing leads, then get disheartened when they end up with nothing at the end. When you are thinking about how much time to invest a week, keep it sustainable.

I always recommend "little consistent action" is far better than massive action once and then nothing for weeks. A great starting point is just one to two hours per day five days a week, and then perhaps a few hours during weekends or evenings to view properties for potential deals! Can you commit to that? Course you can.

No matter how exciting rent-to-rent is, your other time commitments aren't going anywhere. Particularly if you are a busy person with a full-time job and kids, "the more time you spend, the more you get out from it" is a myth. Honestly, it's less about how much time you spend and more about how you're using the time you have. This book is full of tips and tricks to help you be as efficient and productive as possible.

If you set unrealistic goals for how much time and effort you're able to put in, all you are going to do is burn yourself out. This is a marathon, not a sprint – pace yourself. Take into account the other things that you need to do with your week. Building the habit of working on your rent-to-rent projects for just an hour a day is a much more sustainable approach in the long run.

You also need to account for the fact that getting the property itself is just the first step. Once you have got a deal, this is when you need to be prepared to put in the hours. Refurbishing a property in order to let it out – we'll discuss this in Chapter 9 – demands a lot of time – usually 20 to 30 hours for a week or two.

Once the property is set up, you might need to devote a couple of hours or so a day to management. As long as you systemise everything correctly, eventually you shouldn't need to spend more than 15 minutes per day staying on top of things.

This means that you should plan for the demand on your time to scale up as the business does. Fortunately, if your goal is to replace your work income, this means you will have a clear financial marker for when you can start devoting more time to rent-to-rent and reduce the hours you spend working your original day job.

This can be one of the hardest challenges. In reality, many people would prefer to surpass their work income to allow for unexpected costs, reinvestment and tax before taking the leap to quit the day job entirely. Regardless, it's a great first step. Depending on how rough your job is, many people would be prepared to take a slight pay cut to do something they love and reclaim their time for themselves.

CASE STUDY
Scaling your goals step-by-step to keep them achievable

Even if your eventual goal might be to replace your work income and win back your free time, it's not going to happen overnight. Meeting your property, financial and time management goals is a process that starts small and scales up.

Anna is a nurse working 40 hours a week, earning £2,500 per month. Her goal is to start up a rent-to-rent business that will replace her nursing income and allow her to retire. She makes a step-by-step plan that will help her to get up to the point of having replaced her income before she quits her nursing job.

1. One hour per day Mon-Fri sourcing deals in her lunch break. Three hours per week in the evenings or weekends doing viewings.
2. Deal 1 secured. Book four days off work to set up the unit.
3. Deal 1 now cash-flowing £1,000 per month.
4. Deal 2 secured. Book two days off work to set up the unit.
5. Deal 2 cash-flowing £1,000 per month.
6. Total cash-flow is £2,000 per month – Anna is now able to afford working part-time, which frees up more time for her next deals.
7. Deal 3 secured, once set up, it provides a cash flow of £1,000 per month.
8. Anna's total monthly cash flow is now £3,000 – £500 more than her starting income. Anna can now hand in her notice.

By keeping her goals achievable and scaling up with every win, Anna is making sure that she's more likely to achieve them in the long term. If you take this approach yourself, it makes it much easier to go the distance and achieve even the most ambitious goals.

Assess your resources

Getting started with rent-to-rent is certainly much more straightforward than other approaches like buy-to-let. Whilst you don't need to apply for a mortgage, find a big deposit or sit through the lengthy legal processes (all before you even get the keys), you do still need resources to get it done right – whether it's time, money, skills, or help from others.

Working out what you already have and what you still need is the next step.

Money

A lot of the hype around traditional rent-to-rent says that you don't need a penny to get started. Often, this is coming from some property course that will tell you that you can get started for free, then turn around and charge you two grand – leaving you with no money for deals. Nonsense!

Where this money might come from can vary from person to person, including:

- Income from work, investments, or other properties you already own
- Capital available, including savings, inheritance, or equity in your home

If you don't have the money yourself, you are going to need to get help from someone else willing to lend you the money or invest themselves. This might involve:

- Asking friends or family to help you out
- Forming a partnership with someone who has the money, but not the time to run the business
- External loans
- Partnering with a landlord by offering to split the profit if they are willing to let you manage their property

I recommend that you need a minimum investment of around £7,000 to get started for your average rent-to-rent deal. This usually comprises a light cosmetic refurb, furnishing the property, first months rent in advance and potentially a deposit. Sometimes you need less, sometimes more – it depends on the location. I've had deals where all I needed to spend was just £50 for a microwave. I've had other deals cost me as much as £9,000 for converting a property into a licenced HMO!

It's important to remember that we don't own these properties and, therefore, should be careful about investing too much money on someone else's asset. This means no new kitchens and bathrooms unless the landlord is paying!

Something else to consider is, usually when sourcing deals through letting agents, you might need to pass a credit check or have a guarantor (I will talk about this more later).

If you are looking for any additional education and support, this will cost more on top of that.

For example, James works in sales and currently earns £3,000 per month. If

James's goal is to replace his income, and the average deal generates £1,000 net monthly cash flow in return for a £7,000 investment, he could expect to need around £21,000 to do 3 deals (£7,000 x 3).

Luckily, James doesn't actually need that full amount from day one – just enough capital for his first deal. Everything else, he can scale up gradually over time.

Time

Rent-to-rent will take time – it won't happen overnight. Before your first deal, you are going to have to put in a lot of legwork in research, finding properties and viewing properties.

Remember, "little consistent action" is key here. I recommend that you spend an hour a day sourcing deals, around five hours a week. Do this either over your lunch breaks, or wherever you can find the time in your day – a total of around five hours a week. Then allocate another three or so hours a week to doing viewings.

This means that when starting out, you need around eight hours a week dedicated to rent-to-rent and doing deals.

If you can make a minimum investment of seven grand (or have a partner who can invest in your business) and you have at least eight hours a week to spend on making this happen, brilliant. You're in a good position to get started with Rent-to-Rent 2.0.

Skills and support

Doing rent-to-rent successfully demands a huge variety of skills and abilities. Expecting to be an expert in all of them yourself – or to have the capacity to do everything alone – is unrealistic. If you don't know something, you need to work out either how to learn or who can help you with it.

No matter who you are, there will be something that is completely foreign to you. When I started, I was confident with the networking and marketing side of things thanks to my experience in the music industry. I was utterly clueless about property, however, and I was terrible at DIY. I still can't put up a shelf to save my life! Because I recognised that, I knew I had to outsource it. I leant on friends and family for favours and invested in recommended professionals to get the job done right (and quickly).

Now, I can hear your first question – "I don't *know* what skills I need yet? I've never done this before!" Luckily, I've got you covered.

When reading a book like this, have you ever found yourself going "I can do that!" or realising that you wouldn't even know where to begin? Pay attention to that while reading, this will give you a sense of your strengths and weaknesses.

If you come across something that you know will be a weakness – perhaps it is designing a brand or maybe negotiating with landlords – make a note of it. In fact, I've put together a set of resources as part of your action plan in the online resources for this book at http://www.simonsmithonline.com/book-resources.

Working out how you are going to deal with this weakness has to be part of your starting strategy. It doesn't matter if it is educating yourself, getting a mentor to support you, or completely outsourcing it to someone else.

> CASE STUDY
> ### Toby struggled with confidence selling rent–to–rent, so did this instead
>
> Toby is a builder looking to get into the property game. He knows what his strengths are: he's really handy and amazing at DIY. The chance to make a living out of refurbishing and maintaining properties is really exciting for Toby.
>
> Unfortunately, Toby realises he needs to get over his shyness first. He's not really the smoothest talker and his communication skills aren't fantastic. As a result, he is really nervous about pitching rent-to-rent and all the talking he knows he is going to have to do to get deals.
>
> Toby's sister, Juliet, luckily works in Marketing and is confident in presenting. While she doesn't have the time to do all of the legwork, she offers to attend viewings and support with negotiations. Toby and Juliet agree that she'll be the face of the business and Toby will lead on turning the properties around.

To help you with this, I've put a summary of what you need to have achieved at the end of each chapter.

> TEAM-BUILDING
> ### Mentors and masterminds
>
> One of the biggest struggles with any new skill or business is that you just don't know what you don't know, right? Having someone who knows what they're talking about to give you advice and run ideas past can make the difference between succeeding and making costly mistakes.

Rent-to-Rent 2.0 is a very niche and forward-thinking concept that people in your current circle might not understand or support. This was extremely challenging for me at the start and can seed a lot of doubt and anxiety that sadly stops many people from taking action.

The way I navigated this was to keep my plans private, work behind the scenes and align myself with people that did understand until I had proof of concept. It's funny how supportive people will become once you've got some results.

When I was starting out in property, I surrounded myself with people that had already achieved what I wanted to do myself. This led to me acquiring mentors and joining masterminds where I could be around like-minded people. I also had the opportunity to learn from their mistakes, so I didn't have to make my own – the same thing I am trying to do for you by writing this book.

Building your starting strategy

Even if you started today, you won't achieve your financial goals tomorrow. Even getting your first deal within a month might require a lot of work and a little luck. When deciding your next steps, keep them realistic.

I recommend setting yourself several goals spread out over the next 12 to 24 months, a 3-month goal, a 6-month goal, a 12-month goal, and a 24-month goal. As a guide only (set your own goals that fit you best) here is an example of what might be achievable:

- *90 days.* If you are following my advice, getting your first deal within 90 days is achievable. You might not technically be in profit just yet, but you would have successfully secured, set-up and tenanted your property to generate your first taste of cash flow!
- *6 months.* At this point, you could reasonably expect to have found two other deals and started generating cash flow. By now, you might be able to replace a £3,000 monthly work income entirely with income from rent-to-rent.
- *12 months.* You should now be a well-established business. If you have been able to keep scaling over this time, you might be able to hit an income of £10,000 a month.
- *24 months.* Invest in your first property that you own.

Part one: Get prepared with a professional set-up

So, at this point, you should have a slightly better idea of where you are now and what you need to be doing next. Having a better picture means that you don't need to be guessing and improvising all the time. It also lets you have a clearer idea of anything you need to have ready or be prepared for before it's necessary.

Nothing you're deciding here needs to be set in stone. Things might adapt and change as you gain experience and get a better idea of what you're doing. Don't be afraid to come back and update your plans if needed!

One last thing. THINK BIG. Whilst I've made these goals apply to as many people as possible, it's important to understand some of you will only need/want a couple of deals to change your life and hit your goals. Others of you will want massive cash flow and a seven-figure rent-to-rent empire! Whichever category you fall into, remember to push yourself and think big. If your goals don't make you excited and slightly scared, they may not be big enough.

Good luck.

YOU SHOULD HAVE	• A general vision – the motivator that will keep you going when things get tough • Clear and specific goals – achievable milestones that you can use to measure progress and how things are going • An honest assessment of your resources and capabilities – rent-to-rent takes time, money and specific skill sets. You won't have all of them. The sooner you recognise what you need, the sooner you can make a plan to deal with what you don't have

CHAPTER 3

Looking the part: setting up a Rent-to-Rent 2.0 business

It had been a long day of trying to source my first deal and all I had got were no's. When I got home, I slammed the door, threw off my baggy suit and shoes – the closest thing I had to a formal and professional outfit – and crashed onto the sofa like a moody teenager.

"Long day?" Lucy asked.

I faked a smile and nodded defeatedly.

I knew something was wrong, but I didn't know what. I understood the concepts, had my script memorised, I had even purchased a so-called "rent-to-rent agreement" from some guy off Facebook... but I was still being met with the same objections and questions I had no good answer to, time after time.

"How long have you been trading?" *(3 days)*

"What's your website?" "Oh, it's currently down" (*I didn't actually have one*)

"How many properties do you have?" (*1*)

And my personal favourite: "Sorry, the landlord wants a family."

That night, I laid there wide awake: unable to sleep as I went through the problem from every angle. Then it dawned on me; the main objections were all about credibility and I had absolutely none. I was faking it and it was clear to see.

I jumped out of bed, grabbed my laptop and made a list of the key things I had been asked. I researched business set-ups and property management compliance and started implementing everything I learned, one by one.

A week later I had a visible virtual office, a website, a leaflet with my offer and pictures of my first property – my buy-to-let – to showcase my "portfolio" and went back out there.

Suddenly the no's turned into maybe's and the maybe's turned into yes's. A few weeks later, I was close to a deal, I could feel it.

The issue is that many of the mainstream courses on traditional rent-to-rent that I have seen and heard about tend to focus on setting up quickly and immediately getting out there. They don't focus much on how to actually get landlords interested in your services. This leads to a problem: you often find yourself pitching guaranteed rent to sceptical landlords or agents without any credibility or proven experience to back your claims up.

Jumping straight in ends up with you colliding head-first with a massive hurdle. With no professional positioning or credibility, you are offering landlords a deal that sounds "too good to be true" without offering them any reason to trust you.

This is asking a lot of landlords. For many people, their property is their biggest asset. When you are offering to guarantee rent on a property, you are also asking a landlord to take a big risk. They might not have ever heard of rent-to-rent before and you are asking them to trust you with their livelihoods, their pension, or their kids' inheritance.

In rent-to-rent, you are competing with more traditional letting agents. These guys are already positioned as experts: they have an established and credible reputation, physical locations and web presence; they are properly suited and booted; and they have a solid brand to go with it.

Positioning yourself as an expert who knows what you are talking about helps in two ways. It convinces the landlords to take you seriously and that you can offer them a valuable service. It also helps with your mindset and confidence. It is far easier to move forward with direction and momentum once you have already established a professional brand and business presence for yourself.

The first thing I did when I realised this, was to go out and print out a pile of leaflets. These weren't complicated – just a side of A4 paper explaining rent-to-rent and my services. I immediately noticed that going to a viewing and providing the landlord with a brochure to take home and discuss with their partners over the dinner table, meant I was taken far more seriously.

Over time, I started putting more and more into place to establish my brand and professional positioning. In this section I'm going to share what I learned and give you a step by step system to follow to set up the perfect Rent-to-Rent 2.0 business– amazingly, some people have spent tens of thousands on courses and mentors without having been told about any of this! With each step, I noticed that the process of getting deals got easier and easier and I heard "no" less and less.

Building credibility

When you are starting out, it can be difficult to get the first piece of credibility – how can you promise guaranteed rent if you have never done it before? The trick is to work with the experience, authority and network that you *do* have and use it to prove that you know what you are doing.

You might have a contact in the NHS who could provide a constant stream of trainee doctors needing a room near their hospital. A friend might be an interior designer who you could partner up with and offer landlords examples of the finish you give to properties!

Perhaps you have already made some property investments that you can use to you can manage a property. You might have friends or family who already have property that you can use to build experience and establish credibility.

Using this, you can then start to build a narrative positioning yourself as an expert with the know-how to solve the landlord's problems. Being able to say "For these reasons, I promise you that you don't need to worry about managing your property or missing rent payments," is inherently more convincing than a narrative like "I hate my job, I am broke and I need this deal to work out!"

From here, there are several steps that help you back up this more confident narrative with a credible and professional operation.

Create your own Ltd

There are a number of ways you can operate as a business. The one that works best for you will ultimately depend on your specific financial situation and goals. I am not qualified to give accountancy advice – I recommend consulting with an accountant to make sure things are set up correctly and in line with your personal circumstances.

If you are reading this book, however, you want to do Rent-to-Rent 2.0 and generate massive cash flow in the process. This means that setting up your own Ltd will be essential when you start making serious money. You might as well do this sooner rather than later.

Registering itself is remarkably easy. You don't need any external help and everything can be done online. I recommend checking out www.companies-madesimple.com or one of the many other websites dedicated to starting up new limited companies and using the SIC code 68209 (letting and operating of own or leased real estate).

There are three reasons why setting up your own Ltd and registering with Companies House is valuable: credibility, taxes and liability.

Credibility

If you are a registered Ltd, somebody can look you up on the Companies House register and see that you are an official business. They will also see how long you have been established as an Ltd as well.

The longer your company has existed for, the more credible you are. You will always have to deal with the complication of having only been registered for a day. Setting a company up now means you can start building credibility early. This saves you from working uphill to establish your reputation as a Sole Trader and then starting from scratch again four years down the road.

Taxes

In the early days when you have just one or two active deals as a Sole Trader, you might not find it affects your taxes much. However, as you scale, you will quickly find yourself getting pushed into higher personal tax brackets. This can quickly get expensive.

In an Ltd, you only have to pay corporation taxes – which are capped and significantly lower than the higher rates you would pay in personal tax. Rather than having your self-assessment tax pushed into the higher brackets by your profits, you only need to pay tax on the income you choose to pay yourself. Any remaining profit can be reinvested into the business, without costing you as much as it would otherwise.

Liability

In a worst case scenario, you might find yourself financially liable if something goes wrong. If you don't have the money, this could end up with your personal assets getting seized as a result.

As a Sole Trader, you would get in trouble personally and potentially any of your assets might be on the line – even if they were unconnected to your business. In an Ltd however, your personal assets are safeguarded. If any financial liability is incurred, then they can only come after the Ltd for payment.

Once you have your confirmation from Companies House, you can set yourself up a designated business bank account. You want to keep the finances for your business separate from your personal finances. If you don't, you're just asking for a headache later!

Setting up an account specifically for any company finances makes it easier to keep a clear line between what belongs to yourself and what belongs to the business. Whilst you're going through this process, request to set up an additional tax account in which you can start putting away a portion of your profits so you have your tax reserve ready.

TEAM-BUILDING
Accountants

You will now be responsible for submitting your company accounts and confirmation statements, so be sure to instruct a good accountant. They will ensure you comply with the requirements and keep an eye out for Serviced Accommodation income, which is VATABLE when you are set to hit the threshold (unlike residential HMO rent).

Simple steps to creating your brand

One of the hardest decisions in setting up your Ltd in my experience is choosing the name and business structure. I recommend having one Ltd and two trading names under the same Ltd: one targeting landlords and agents and the other targeting guests and tenants.

Choosing an Ltd name
I believe that there are four approaches to choosing a name for your business:

- A literal name that does what it says on the tin: Pizza Hut
- An abstract name with positive connotations: Apple
- Something connected to your own name or another personal connection: Ford Motor Company
- A name that suggests the values of a company: Diamond

Once you have brainstormed potential names, you then check if it is available for you to use:

1. Check on Companies House to make sure it is available as a Ltd
2. Check that the name – or some variation – is available to register as a web domain for creating a website
3. Do an extensive Google search to make sure that it is an original idea and nobody else is already using something similar in your vicinity

Now you have set up your Ltd, it is time to turn our attention to the two trading names. Brands work best when they are focused. The needs of landlords and tenants are different, therefore trying to target both at once simply won't work. Trying to please everyone at once ends up pleasing nobody.

When starting out, the first thing you need is a property. This means that your first priority is to create a brand aimed at landlords and letting agents. Once you have the property deals, you can begin targeting the guests and tenants.

Keep this in mind when you are designing your branding and choosing the right trading names.

For example: Richard is starting out and trying to work out a name that will capture the brand he wants to target landlords with. The name he settles on uses the first naming strategy – "Secure Rental Management" – his goal is to appeal to landlords looking for safety and security.

When he turns his attention to targeting SA guests later, he chooses "Home Away From Home" for that aspect of his branding.

Defining the customer avatar

As I have already mentioned, the brand itself should be as focused as possible. This means that you can create something convincing and persuasive to your specific target audience, rather than something bland and generic that disappears in the crowd.

To do this, you have to create several "avatars" that represent your ideal customers. I recommend using a maximum of three for one brand in order to keep the brand focused and effective.

Three landlord avatars of Rent-to-Rent 2.0

In Chapter 4, 5, and 6, I will talk you through the research that can help you build your customer avatars. Here are examples of three profiles of landlords that you might target.

Sanj – the accidental landlord

Sanj never expected to be a landlord – his position as a director is more than enough for him. When his parents passed away, he found himself inheriting their home. After Sanj ran the numbers, he realised that it made more sense for him to rent it out rather than sell.

Sanj is now getting increasingly frustrated with how much time and attention it takes to maintain his second property. All he wants is a passive source of income that takes care of itself while he focuses on his career.

Jamie – the retiring professional landlord

Jamie has made a career in property for 30 years now. He is proud of his small empire, but he is now in his late 60s with ten different properties to look after. Jamie is looking to step back a bit in order to focus on other projects, but he doesn't want to lose the income.

What Jamie is looking for is someone who he can trust to manage his properties for him, freeing his hands up to try other things.

Amy and Paul – the overworked professionals

At 38, Amy and Paul's insane work ethic has paid off in spades for them. They have managed to pay off the mortgage on their home and they have somehow afforded a second property. Their plan is to benefit from the passive income, then gift it to their daughter to get her started on the property

---

> ladder when she moves out.
>
> However, they are both just too busy to run it themselves. They need help making sure the property stays maintained and in good condition while providing an income.

Everything in the brand – the colours, the name, the copy, and the website – needs to be tailored towards the customer avatars you have identified.

Creating a logo

Once you've got a name you're happy with and a better idea of who you're targeting, you need a logo. This is something you're probably going to need a hand with if you don't have any graphic design experience.

To get in touch with a graphic designer who can make a decent logo for you, check out websites like www.fiverr.com (or www.99designs.co.uk if you want to go the extra mile). At this point, I recommend not going overboard. This could cost you thousands. I recommend not spending anything more than £100 at this point.

In my case, my first logo was strong, but basic. After a couple of years, once the business was more established, I invested significantly more to rebrand.

Building your website

Having a website you can refer people to is a powerful tool to help even sceptical landlords buy into the idea of rent-to-rent. When I was starting out, I used leaflets, but the question I kept getting was "what's your website?" Not having a website today is like what not having a business card was like a few decades ago: sloppy and unprofessional.

This was true when I started and today it is only more so – your website is your passport to success. Without one, you simply will not be taken seriously.

Besides this, it's a fantastic way to not only command credibility, but to also attract new leads. Today most of my leads come directly from my website, which becomes easier to find on search engines every day.

In Chapter 6, I will talk more about presenting the opportunity while talking with landlords, however, the key is to inform without overwhelming. A well-made website targeting landlords helps inform them as to what rent-to-rent is and how they benefit from your support.

Typically this means that to start with, all your website needs is the following:

- A landing page which makes it clear what you do
- A "how it works" section that breaks things down into simple to understand steps
- A call to action to contact you

This doesn't have to be anything amazingly fancy yet. Making it "perfect" can be done later. Either you can do it yourself – simple templates for web design can be found on www.squarespace.com – or you can allocate a budget to it and hire a freelancer as you did with the logo design.

Once you are established, your website can grow from there. For example, you could showcase a portfolio of properties you maintain or testimonials from landlords. Your first and most important step is creating something to help a landlord process what exactly you are offering and potentially answer all the tricky frequently-asked-questions.

Professional contact details

No matter what background the landlord has, they are going to expect a professional service. This means that looking like a one-man-band who runs their own business out of a van with their mobile can sometimes count against you.

On the other hand, setting up an Ltd comes with a virtual office on Oxford Street. However, people will wonder why you're operating from W1 in London if you are working with property in Lancaster. They will much prefer to talk with a local business.

When I was starting, I would have people not take me seriously when I gave them my mobile number. They would ask "Are you just on your own? What is this organisation?" So, I had to sit down and work out how to present myself more credibly to them.

What I realised was that thanks to my home internet installation, I was already paying for my own landline that I never used. I bought a cheap landline handset and used it to discover what my landline number was. Once I had that, I could update the number on my website to my local landline.

This made all the difference. Whilst it took time for my phone to start ringing, it gave me the perception of a more established outfit – nothing else in my branding had changed! A quick call to Virgin and my landline was redirected to my mobile phone.

Similarly, a professional-looking email is painless to set up, but makes a lot of difference in creating a professional image. Landlords are far more likely to trust an email like "yourname@brandname.com" than your personal email address from when you were a teenager. Imagine how an experienced executive would react to seeing "ladiesman99", "amybaby1234" or "myfishdied" @ hotmail.com " on a business card!

On the other hand, a professional-sounding email address with a local number and website address will convince even the most traditional of landlords that you are running a serious operation.

Official registrations

As a business that will be collecting and storing data on people while managing properties you don't own, there are still some important official governing bodies you need to register with to become compliant. Getting this done right is important. If you don't, rather than finding yourself "financially free", you could find yourself locked up!

ICO registration

The Information Commissioner's Office (ICO) is the first place you need to get registered. Organisations that process personal data are subject to the General Data Protection Regulation (GDPR) and the Data Protection Act 2018. Under the Data Protection (Charges and Information) Regulations 2018 (the Regulations) they must also pay an annual data protection fee, unless they are exempt. You are going to be collecting a lot of information on landlords, tenants, or guests. Better to get this out of the way now.

Registering is easy. Go to ico.org.uk/registration/new and fill out the online form.

Redress scheme sign-up

Back in 2014, the government put legislation in place which requires all property managers and letting agents to join a government-approved redress scheme. Their main purpose is to help resolve or settle complaints from tenants who have suffered loss due to the actions of a property management company who is a member of the scheme.[3]

Since this covers anyone managing a property they don't own, this now includes you! At the time of writing, there are three schemes to choose from:

- The Ombudsman – Property Services (www. ombudsman-services.org/property.html)
- The Property Ombudsman (www.tpos.co.uk)
- The Property Redress Scheme (PRS) (www.theprs.co.uk)

Of these, I recommend joining the Property Redress Scheme. However, since this is an annual membership, don't worry too much about joining until you're ready to start sourcing deals. While you do need to sign up, work smart and look after the pennies, right?

Set up business insurance
Having business insurance is an important part of protecting you and your business. Now, I am not an insurance broker and this can get complicated and change a lot as your business grows or evolves – you should check what you need specifically with an insurance broker – however, here is a good place to start:

- Public Liability Insurance – It doesn't matter how big a company is or what it does – it needs public liability insurance. This protects the business if a client or member of the public claims they have been injured or their property damaged, because of your business activities. It's important to note here you will need a separate insurance policy per property to cover individual guests and tenants for additional cover.
- Professional Indemnity Insurance – This is intended to cover you against claims regarding any advice, ideas, tuition, or anything else that cost the landlord money and result in them trying to sue you. Now, you don't really give advice in rent-to-rent, however it is a useful way to cover yourself if someone *thinks* you have. It's also good to have in case you get into other aspects of property like sourcing deals for other people.

3   FAQ. (n.d.). Property Redress Scheme. Retrieved August 7, 2023, from https://www.theprs.co.uk/FAQ

As your business grows and scales, you'll generally want to get other forms of insurance as well. Keep an eye on this, but for the moment, let's keep it simple.

Prepare any legal documents and agreements

Having the correct legal agreements and contracts is an important part of protecting yourself and the landlords or tenants you work with. It can be tempting to wait to get these sorted out until you need them (I'll talk more about negotiating and signing agreements in Chapter 8), but it makes your life so much easier to have them ready ahead of time.

One benefit is that it makes you look more prepared and professional in front of landlords. Having a drafted agreement with you allows you to show a copy to landlords so they can see how the deal will be structured for instance.

You'll need four types of agreement prepared:

- Landlord agreements – This is the agreement you will use to formalise your arrangement with landlords. This should include guaranteed rent details, liability and have the appropriate termination clauses for you to exit the deal should it not work for any reason.
- Letting agent agreements – Whilst in many cases agents will want to use their own agreements, it's essential to get educated regarding Company Let agreements and know which clauses to add, remove and edit.
- Tenant agreements – Tenancies are regulated by the Housing Act of 1988 – you need to use what's called an Assured Shorthold Tenancy (AST).
- Guest agreements – This will usually be provided by the Online Travel Agent (Airbnb for example) when the guest reserves online. However, you will need agreements for all direct bookings as well as terms and conditions for your guests.

Like with insurance, this is a topic I recommend getting professional advice for. When writing up and finalising your agreements, get a lawyer to check everything over. Particularly for additional clauses like liability and what happens in case of termination. (We'll talk more about these in Chapter 8).

If you want to avoid the mistake I made by trusting a randomer on Facebook – and save yourself thousands in the process – you can get access to my agreement templates at http://www.simonsmithonline.com/book-resources.

Part one: Get prepared with a professional set-up

All the work involved in setting up an official business and building a brand pays off in spades. It might be technically possible to get rent-to-rent deals as a sole trader who just turns up at a viewing, but this is the exception not the rule and simply will not allow you to scale. The earlier you start establishing yourself as a business, the better.

Having a proper Ltd and a good brand that targets the landlords you want gives you an automatic head start on building credibility and trust with them. They can look you up and get their heads around rent-to-rent at their own pace – rather than being asked to trust a stranger on the spot at a viewing.

Now you have your business and branding up and running, it's time to start looking for your perfect investment area!

	• Your own Ltd set up
	• A bank account for your Ltd
	• An established landlord brand – with business name and logo
YOU SHOULD HAVE	• A website – doesn't have to be fancy yet, but something you can share with landlords and agents
	• Contact details for your business – including a professional email and a local contact number
	• Official registrations – including ICO, redress scheme, and business insurance
	• Official agreements and documents – including landlord agreements and tenant agreements

CHAPTER 4

Do your homework

Before you can begin finding properties and deals, you need to make your mind up about what kind of rent-to-rent you are planning to operate. In my experience, there are several different approaches:

- Renting out an entire property to a family
- House in Multiple Occupation (Rent-to-HMO) – house-sharing that rents on a room-by-room basis.
- Serviced Accommodation (Rent-to-SA) – renting properties out on a nightly basis, the most famous platform for which being Airbnb.
- Rent-to-Rent 2.0 aka 'The Hybrid Approach' – rather than operating a service dedicated to HMO or SA, a hybrid approach keeps the tools and resources on hand to do either depending on the property and landlord.

I recommend avoiding renting out the entire property on a long term traditional let. Whilst in some instances it can work well, it is far riskier due to the lower profit margins, insurmountable void periods and it often takes longer to break even.

What usually happens in more traditional rent-to-rent is people focus on either HMO or SA. They either chase the safer recurring monthly income from HMO or the big lump (but at times unpredictable) sums of cash from SA.

In Rent-to-Rent 2.0, I recommend the hybrid approach. If you specialise in HMO or SA, you will find that not every property would work out. A hybrid approach gives you far more flexibility in acquiring properties – letting you scale quicker. It makes looking at properties a question of "not if, but how?".

In other words, each time you look at a property it is often a question of *how* you can make it work, not *if* you can make it work. A property that might not be a good investment as an HMO might have features that could make it a valuable SA for example. Of course there are other key factors such as location and condition which can mean a deal is unsuitable.

Having the infrastructure and resources to operate with a hybrid approach also gives you more flexibility too. If an HMO property has all the rooms empty, I might try to get some Airbnb bookings to offset the costs. On the other hand, if I realise that the number of SA properties I have in an area are leading to oversaturation (if a specific area only gets 1,000 bookings per annum, that isn't going to change if I have four or five active Airbnb's), I might convert it to an HMO so I can maximise my profits.

TOP TIP
Don't operate HMO and SA in the same house

Whilst in some scenarios it can be a great advantage to have a property that can work for both SA and HMO, I never recommend mixing the two at the same time. Long-term tenants that call their house a home will rarely seek to share their space with different short-term guests that may or may not respect the property.

As I had chosen my hometown as my investment area, I had an easy leg-up when I started doing rent-to-rent there. Having the local knowledge meant I didn't have to overthink anything. I knew where would work well for students, professionals, or any other tenant avatars.

To start off, my strategy was to stay close to the city centre. My first ever rent-to-rent deal was an HMO in what was pretty much the perfect location. It was a stone's throw away from the city centre, close to the University and near a lovely park. It was a complete no-brainer – who wouldn't want to live there? This allowed me the potential of attracting both professional and student tenants.

Ultimately, this is the trick to HMO. You need to be asking yourself "where would people like to live?" and then look for properties which match your tenant avatar's needs. SA requires a different question: "where would people want to stay on a short-term basis and why?"

My second rent-to-rent deal was a little trickier. It was a super-strict contract with a letting agent – I had no termination clause and the break clause meant I had to stay with it for at least a year (I'll talk more about this in Chapter 8). I had to make it work.

However, the issue was that it was a smaller two bedroom property. The more rooms there are to let, the more successful an HMO typically is and the more potential for profit. With just two rooms, it was impossible to see how to make the numbers work.

So, I decided to look into running this property – my second rent-to-rent deal – as SA. When I started telling people that I was going to run this deal as a serviced accommodation, they couldn't believe it. I would get told "bro, you're talking about Airbnb in this town? This isn't LA!"

One of the key parts of setting up an SA is getting your channel manager: a central management system which SA providers like Airbnb, Booking.com, or Expedia can connect to. This automates everything so they can talk to each other without you needing to do everything manually. When I called one of the biggest channel managers in the UK to get me set up, they actually told me – after tapping away for a while – I was the first operator on their portal to have ever come to them from that city!

I said to myself "mate, you are either a pioneer doing something for the first time and this is really smart... or this is the stupidest thing I've ever done. If I get this wrong, I'm finished." I went for it.

I ended up getting guests flooding in. Someone in town for graduation. Money-in: £500. A house round the corner floods and the insurance needs to find them a place to stay for two months. Boom! Seven grand. International students from China and executives from Rolls Royce... it became quickly clear that this would work out.

I actually ended up taking advantage of this flexibility for most HMOs I acquired. I would put my properties on Airbnb to see if I could get a sexy five week booking. If I got lucky, I could often make my initial investment back in a flash with an SA. Then I would shift to an HMO to settle down and enjoy the recurring income while moving the money into the next place.

Now that's Rent-to-Rent 2.0!

Where should you start looking for properties?

Particularly when starting out with rent-to-rent, I think it is important to stay as close to home as possible. A concept that is important to Rent-to-Rent 2.0 is what I call "the Rent-to-Rent Radius". Basically, you want to be operating rent-to-rent locally to where you live. I recommend that you focus on finding properties within 20 miles of home – ideally within five miles. The closer, the better.

There are several reasons why operating close to home is useful. My three top reasons are local knowledge, credibility and ability to source properties easily.

If you are a local, you know the area inside out already. This means that you don't need to do as much research to work out what makes a property effective in the area or what tenants might be interested in.

This local knowledge can be used for leverage in your marketing or while dealing with landlords or agents. As a savvy local who knows the area, you are automatically far more credible straight off the bat than some investor who doesn't know where anything is.

Finally, the last thing you want is to end up needing to drive for an hour or two both ways every time you need to attend a viewing of a potential new deal or every time there is a small issue. Whereas if you are within the rent-to-rent radius range, it is far easier. My first rent-to-rent property is ten doors down from my own place, my second is about five minutes walk in the opposite direction. Anything that needs my personal attention is a breeze to get to.

I learnt the benefit of this when I did such a good job for a woman locally that she asked me if I operated in London. Of course I said I did – it was a sweet deal in a banging area in West Kensington, the potential profits were amazing. However, I quickly started to realise that the hassle of needing to get in and out of London quickly ate into those profits and more importantly what little free time I did have during this phase.

Once you're established, you will have the systems set up and know how you can manage your portfolio remotely. On top of this, you'll have a team whose job it is to make sure things run smoothly. At this point, expanding beyond the rent-to-rent radius could absolutely work. But, just accept that it's always going to be easier to operate rent-to-rent the closer you are to home. FACT.

Just picking any old property nearby isn't good enough though. If you want a property to generate cash flow for you, it needs to check certain boxes first. In order to find this out, you're going to have to do some market research.

Luckily, I've discovered a few secrets to share on what to look for in a winning deal and how to check if a property will meet your needs as easily and efficiently as possible.

What to consider in market research

When looking at an area, there is a lot to consider that will be useful in considering the value of a property and how it could be used in rent-to-rent. Through personal experience, I have worked out the key considerations that will help you work out if rent-to-rent will work out in the area:

- The client avatar
- The macro area
- The more specific "green flags" in the area

These help to reduce the learning curve and let you assess an area for good properties in a quick and effective manner. In fact, in my years of doing deals and coaching countless people, I have never had a situation where these key considerations were carefully considered and we were not able to make it work out.

Client avatar

Before you start looking around aimlessly at random properties, you need to think about who you are trying to appeal to. In Chapter 3, I talked about customer avatars, specifically landlord avatars. At this point, you need to consider your tenant and guest avatars.

An SA guest or an HMO tenant are going to be interested in very different things. This might affect everything from how many bedrooms or bathrooms are needed, whether there is parking, or something as simple as budget and expected quality of the property itself.

Knowing who your tenants are lets you work out what you need to source the ideal deal.

Suggested client avatar – the student

When dealing with students, there are several things which many will have in common:

1. They either won't have a car or might not afford to run one
2. They will need a space to study at home
3. They will want to be as close to university campus as possible
4. Students don't need to pay council tax

As a result, a property that would work well as an HMO for students is going to have these as standard:

1. Within easy walking distance of the University (and/or the city centre and nightlife!)
2. There doesn't need to be available parking for each room
3. Every single room will need its own desk and study space
4. The property itself will need decent high-speed internet
5. Because you won't be paying council tax, you can be more flexible on price – you can afford to pay the landlord a little more and still make money on the property

Other client avatars might include:

1. The professional tenant
2. The weekend-breakers
3. The holiday-makers
4. The corporate client
5. The construction company

An important consideration for any tenant avatar, however, is the quality of the property. It might feel obvious to point out, but many rent-to-renters will often look at getting the cheapest deals – without doing the market research first. They then end up with the properties that may not fit the requirements of their target audience.

One of the key things that I have learnt with Rent-to-Rent 2.0 is that I can always make a high quality property work for me, somehow. Generally, most tenants will be far happier with a higher quality property and you'll have an easier time filling a nicer place.

When looking at the area itself, I recommend analysing and researching both the area in general and the specific amenities, facilities and other major locations and businesses nearby.

Macro area

Before delving deeper into the specifics of what might appeal to a tenant, you have to work out if there is any room for a rent-to-rent business in your area. To do this, you need to find out how many properties there are available to let in your area.

Depending on your goals, building your portfolio of rent-to-rent properties may require a large supply of rental properties in the area. When the number of properties is below a certain number, it suggests that there simply aren't enough potential deals in the area. If, for example, it turns out that you are in the middle of nowhere with just twelve properties available to LET, clearly it will be hard to build a seven-figure revenue business. It may, however, be fine if you only want one or two deals.

In my experience, the absolute bare minimum is 50 available properties – if it is over 200, then that's fantastic. Lots of people might put a ton of energy into looking for some kind of "perfect" goldmine of rent-to-rent deals. However, what I recommend is to just start with one deal. If that works, then keep doing deal after deal, one after another, until things slow down. Then you just change the area. I've had to do this a number of times – it's how you end up being able to scale really big without oversaturating your own area.

How you find out the number of properties for let in an area is simple – you look it up on an online property portal. If you go online and search for properties for let, you'll get back a rough number of the properties available. Where I am based has around 400 available, which is OK. Manchester, when I last checked, had roughly over a thousand properties, which is fantastic.

Online Property Portals

These websites are where landlords or letting agents post properties for sale or rent and tenants or buyers go to find a property to rent or buy. Which one you use depends on your local area – popular ones in the UK include Rightmove or Zoopla.

Ten property-filling "green flags" you need to know about

Once you know whether the area has an adequate number of available properties, the next step is working out whether you'll be able to fill the properties themselves. Whether you're doing SA or HMO, I have worked out a list of ten key factors to consider. Each of these factors are a potential green flag for any nearby properties – the more there are, the more attractive the property might be to potential clients.

1 – Major cities
The bigger the city is, the greater the demand will be for both HMOs and SA in general.

In this case, anything within a five-mile radius counts! For each of the other property fillers, it should be within roughly a mile – basically, walking distance – and easily accessible to count positively. This is because unless the property filler is a big attraction with a big pull, most people want to be as close to it as possible and will often search via maps for the most local properties.

2 – Major transport links
A well-connected property is always valuable. It makes it easier to access and could make things like commuting far more attractive and easier. If you are in a bigger city, this means looking for a good bus network or things like being close to a London Underground station.

On a higher level, this also involves more long-distance travel links. Major train stations are particularly valuable – especially if your tenant or guest avatar might travel to London often.

Being close to airports is also very helpful. An HMO might appeal to pilots or flight attendants. Running an SA would also likely get a lot of one-night bookings from guests who want to be next to the airport for an early flight or for those looking for a place to stay if they arrive late in the evening.

3 – Large businesses or employers
Even if you would otherwise consider an area to be in the middle of nowhere, a large business having a base of operations nearby is going to draw a lot of HMO tenants and SA guests. Examples might be an Amazon distribution centre or some sort of major factory or significant manufacturing facility.

This means that a large proportion of any HMOs in the area might have professionals working for that business as tenants. In addition, any visiting executives visiting for business trips will want to find conveniently placed short-term accommodation to stay in while they are in town.

In my area, a good example is Rolls Royce. Everyone in town seems to be directly connected with someone from Rolls Royce, in fact it feels like half the local workforce is actually employed by them! On top of this, I've had German executives for Rolls Royce book stays of up to six weeks in my SA units before.

To discover the largest employers in your area, google is your friend. "Biggest employers in Cardiff" for example will tell you who the biggest employers in that city are. From there, you can work out where their offices are and which general areas of town might be most conveniently located.

4 – Hospitals
I find that being close to a hospital makes both HMOs and SAs work. From an SA perspective, you might get people looking for short-term accommodation while visiting friends or family in the hospital. Once again, the closer the better. I've got a number of properties a stone throw away from the local hospital and guests are so grateful to be able to pop across the road for multiple daily visiting hours without having to worry about parking and so on.

On top of this, a huge number of NHS staff relocate to the UK from abroad. These professionals are often on healthy salaries and need accommodation near the hospital, however, they often want to try before they buy.

This means that they look for room shares in convenient HMOs or temporary short-term accommodation. After six months or so and they are certain about their preferred area, they typically fly their families over and move into their own place.

5 – Construction projects
Areas in which there is a lot of construction often represent fantastic opportunities. Significant construction or redevelopment work might continue for a number of years, during which time the workers will need to remain near the site.

It's possible to make an entire Rent-to-Rent 2.0 business on construction accommodation alone. Companies would prefer to put their teams in houses to enjoy kitchen facilities and communal spaces to relax rather than months on end in hotels eating at local restaurants and having to order drinks at expensive hotel bars.

6 – Tourism opportunities
This point will apply more when looking at how suitable a property is for SA. Significant tourism in the area is likely to draw a regular supply of guests. Whether it's a sports stadium, theme park, or that your city hosts an annual event, these attractions can create a massive influx of guests.

Major festivals can be extremely lucrative for SA operators. They ensure that there is a guaranteed period in the year in which demand for accommodation will go through the roof for up to a fortnight. This increased demand also means that you could make a mint if you raise your prices to match!

7 – Universities

What I call "rent-to-student" properties are often a great opportunity to absolutely smash it. A big city will generally have at least one university and a constant stream of students looking for accommodation. On top of this, a student residence doesn't need to pay council tax at all – as I mentioned earlier, this is a great chance to save a few pennies and get a bit more profit out of a property.

In the past, I have taken a student property, given it a lick of paint and got it back up to scratch, then been able to rent it out for nearly three times what the landlord had been able to charge for it. Everybody is happy – the students get a great place to live, the landlord receives a guaranteed rent without needing to lift a finger, and I make a tidy profit.

On top of this, a student who realises that they can get a great room from you *will* recommend you to everyone else. My fifth rent-to-rent deal, I put an HMO up on Spareroom.com and had a Chinese student contact me. Since they were having a lot of trouble communicating in English, they had been having a rough time finding accommodation in town.

Almost immediately after I had managed to get them sorted out with the room and the deposit paid, my WhatsApp started blowing up. Nearly 20 other Chinese students were messaging me about houses and I ended up getting 16 rooms filled for a year in just a day!

The icing on the cake was that a bunch of them insisted on paying for the entire year up front in cash! The bank looked at me like I was crazy when I went in with 24 grand in cash to deposit in my bank account – it took nearly an hour to sort out! Even after we had paid tax on this insane windfall, it really supercharged the business!

8 – Hotels and commercial buildings

Businesses like hotels, fast food restaurants, or supermarkets are dependent on having a strong customer base near enough to justify the location. This means that if you find a location with high-class hotels or huge supermarkets and shopping centres nearby, you can be confident that there is going to be demand – the research has already been done for you!

9 – Premium location access

Desirable areas will always attract people that want to live there, as well as others who would love to visit. This means if you can secure properties in premium locations you will never be short of property demand! Plus another advantage is that you will also be able to charge a premium for the pleasure.

10 – Social hotspots

Every city has its social hotspots with cool shops, trendy coffee spots and trendy bars. These will attract both HMO tenants and SA guests that may not want to stay in the most obvious city centre locations, but like the affluence of a suburban area that offers a trendy lifestyle. Look out for these!

The Ideal Deal

We've covered client avatars, your investment area and green flags to look out for, but now let's take a look at "Ideal Deal". In other words, the key criteria as to what makes a good rent-to-rent property. Firstly, as a general rule, I've found my best property deals are in overall good condition and only require light cosmetic refurbishment. I am also an advocate of modern properties with better fixtures and fittings, and superior energy efficiency.

As the criteria varies depending on whether you are targeting SA or HMO, I have given you three additional criteria for each:

Serviced Accommodation

Property Size

After doing years of market research, one clear thing has become apparent: the larger the property, the less competition. It's a case of simple economics: if there is more of a certain type of property available, you are going to have to work harder to compete for those precious bookings.

This is why I have found it best to avoid studios and one-bed properties, as you are competing with hotel giants that have the economies of scale, in-house cleaning teams and superior linen management, which makes it impossible to compete on price. Two-bed properties have become increasingly popular with SA providers and, therefore, competition is also fierce; so be selective.

With three, four and five bed properties, competition will be minimal and not only will you get more bookings, but you will be able to charge a premium as your offering will be so much more appealing than five hotel rooms.

Apartments vs Houses

If I've said it once, I've said it a thousand times... 'Houses beat apartments every day of the week'. Houses are typically more spacious, benefit from their own entrance, offer more privacy and as a result, I've found them easier to manage as they cause less disruption to neighbours.

Another key consideration is that most apartments are leasehold and, therefore, must adhere to the terms of the head lease. Unfortunately, these often restrict the operation of short-term lets and, therefore, would not work for the rent-to-rent business model.

I've heard horror stories of uneducated rent-to-renters making the costly mistake of entering into an agreement, investing thousands, to learn within just a few weeks of operation, that serviced accommodation is prohibited, and the landlord has had to terminate with immediate effect, leaving them in a £6,000 hole.

Not good…

Parking

Whether you are a tourist, in the area for family or a corporate booking, parking is always important. Off-road and gated secure parking is even more desirable! I even have properties where parking is such a premium that we charge for additional parking options!

As a general rule, I only recommend acquiring a property without parking in a very central location when it is in close proximity to key transport links. If there is permit parking, this can work but will take more organisation, but can definitely be worth it for the right property.

House in Multiple Occupancy

Licensed versus unlicensed

When acquiring HMO properties, you have two options:

1. To focus on properties that already have an HMO licence. These properties will already meet the health and safety requirements, and will often come fully furnished meaning your initial outlay will be significantly lower.
2. To target properties that are suitable to convert into HMOs. This means they will have to be suitable in terms of the number of rooms and the layout.

I have done both and can recommend that if you have a lower budget, it may be advisable to aim for existing HMO-licences. However, some of my most profitable deals have been conversions. Remember, if you intend on converting a property into an HMO, you must check with your local council to ensure there is no Article 4 direction in your area.

Size of rooms

As HMO tenants are renting a room and all other areas are shared, the size of personal space is important. This means good HMOs often have spacious bedrooms that allow for adequate living space and storage. You will also find you will be able to charge a higher rent for larger rooms, therefore, increasing your cash flow.

> TOP TIP
> ## Check with your local council!
> Check with your local council to ensure all room sizes in the property meet their minimum requirements. They will also stipulate the necessary room sizes and amenities for communal space, depending on the number of occupants.

Number of bathrooms

In an HMO, the greater the bathroom-to-tenant ratio, the more desirable the property. Let's face it, who wants to live in a property where you share the bathroom with five strangers? As we are not in the business of adding bathrooms to properties we don't own, it's important to target properties with as many bathrooms as possible. Another key factor to look out for is properties with en-suite bedrooms, as they tend to demand the highest rents.

One last thing. Another key detail often overlooked is that rent-to-rent works best when the landlord does not have a mortgage on the property. This gives us the freedom to legally sublet the property and operate SA or HMO more simply. Believe it or not around 38 per cent of UK homes are owned outright, so it's a lot more common than you think.[4] It's, therefore, essential to find out if the landlord has a mortgage before moving forward with any deal.

If yes, the landlord must check that the terms allow the rent-to-rent business model (be it SA or HMO), obtain consent from their lender, or change onto the correct mortgage product. Now, I'm not qualified to give mortgage

---

4   Steed, K. (2023, June 7). UK Mortgage Statistics 2023 – Mortgage Facts and Stats Report. Uswitch. Retrieved September 4, 2023, from https://www.uswitch.com/mortgages/mortgage-statistics/

advice so please always consult with a mortgage advisor before completing any rent-to-rent deal.

If you follow the guidance laid out, your "Ideal Deal" will be around the corner. But remember other than the legalities, these criteria are there to guide you only, and are not set in stone. I've had deals that didn't follow my criteria entirely, but have still been successful, so remember any deal that you are confident will generate you cash flow should be considered.

Getting clarity on the kinds of deals you want

Once you have done the market research, you need to get a feel for the figures and make sure your deals are going to stack! Remember, the first rule of investment is "DON'T LOSE MONEY!", so doing the legwork here can be make a big difference – it saves you from wasting your time on deals that simply won't work and having the figures already prepared and clear in your head helps you present yourself as a competent professional when talking to the owner.

I have developed a simple and straightforward ten-minute exercise to develop this clarity – a competent competition calculator. There are two versions of this, one for running an HMO and another for an SA. Since in Rent-to-Rent 2.0 we want the flexibility of operating with a hybrid approach, I recommend doing both to help you decide whether a property might work better as an HMO or an SA. You can download my competition calculators at http:// www.simonsmithonline.com/book-resources.

Calculate the average guaranteed rent

First, you need to get an idea of the average guaranteed rent in the area. In a nutshell, what you do is go onto your local online property portal and work out the average market rent of properties in your area. Find at least ten properties for each number of bedrooms (so at least ten two-bedroom properties, three beds, four beds and so on) and tally up the rent prices. Then divide the total by the number of properties to find the average rent for that size of property.

For example, you go onto your local property portal and search for all three bed properties in your area. If the sum total of the first ten rents is £15,820, then your local average rent for a three bedroom property is £1,582 a month (£15,820 divided by ten).

Calculate for HMO profitability
The process for working out the average HMO room rate is very similar. Look on a local property online platform specialising in house shares, such as spareroom.co.uk, using at least ten rooms in your local area, and find your local average room rate.

If you multiply this average room rate by the number of rooms in a property, you can then work out the average rent you would *receive* from the HMO – if all the rooms were full. When analysing a deal to see if it stacks, I have found that it's not so much about the potential net cash flow when all rooms are let: you have to account for some empty rooms.

In high-demand areas I have been satisfied with breaking even with one room empty, as I know there will be minimal voids. This is especially true when operating a student HMO as you are likely to get a whole group signing for the year.

However, in areas where I am less certain of tenant demand, I have found being as close as possible to breaking even with 1.5 to 2 rooms empty is optimum. This means that if one room is empty, you are profitable. If two rooms are empty, you would still break even or minimise your losses.

If you are not breaking even with between one and two rooms empty, this means that the property may be unsuitable for HMO and it will make it harder for you to make a profit! In this case, explore SA figures for the same deal before moving onto the next one.

> Peter has found a potential deal in a prime student location with a monthly market rent of £1,000 for a four bed property, and that he can charge £600 a month for a room. Is it a deal? He is confident he will find a group of four students that will let the property for the entire year and, therefore, is satisfied with breaking even with one room empty and a likely minimum cash flow of £600 pcm. He deducts this amount from total potential income of £2,400 (£600 x 4) leaving £1,800.
> After deducting the guaranteed rent of £1,000 and leaving £600 for bills, Peter decides the deal stacks and will in fact generate £800 net cash flow!

Calculate for SA profitability
The process for SA is very similar. Look on Airbnb to find the nightly rates for a property of the size you are investigating. From there, calculate the average

nightly rate. In SA, the reality is you will not be booked 100 per cent of the time and, therefore, a safe approach is to only take deals where you can break even at 50 per cent occupancy – your target is the net nightly rate multiplied by 15. If you break even at 50 per cent occupancy after removing bills and the guaranteed rent, then the property is a good deal for SA.

This takes out a lot of the risk and increases the likelihood of cash flow. Remember, rule 1: do not lose money!

> Peter decides to explore his options by calculating whether operating the property as an SA would be a better deal. After looking on Airbnb, he estimates that the average net nightly rate would be £1500 a night. Assuming he can rent it out around 50 per cent of the time, this will be at least £2250 a month.
>
> Once the bills and guaranteed rent are removed, Peter stands to make £650 in profit, and that's on a bad month! At a more realistic occupancy rate of 80 per cent, Peter stands to make £2000 net profit!

Once you have done the maths for your area, keep these in the front of your mind. It is going to be essential in the next steps. Once you start viewing properties, speed is the name of the game. You want to have the confidence to be able to place an offer on the spot and to negotiate with authority. Having done the research and being able to quote the numbers means you don't have to waste time working out if a deal is going to be worth it – you'll already know.

YOU SHOULD HAVE

- Potential tenant avatars you want to target
- Research showing the key factors that influence which tenant and guest avatars might be interested in the area
- An average estimate of property prices in the area, separated by size of property
- An average estimate of HMO and SA prices in the area
- Calculations working out potential cash flow from properties in the area

PART TWO

Sourcing and closing the perfect deal

I know what you're thinking... "Get on with it already", "When do I step foot in a property?", "Give me the cash flow". I get it, but trust me you have to lay the foundations before you can build the house. The good news is that you have taken the first steps towards establishing yourself as a professional expert offering a valuable service:

- You have clear goals and objectives
- You have an Ltd which will become more and more credible over time
- You have done the work to understand your local area
- You have crunched the numbers and know what you are looking for in a property

Having done all this first means that you are far more prepared for anything that you might come up against in the next stages of the process. Now it is time to start uncovering leads and getting property deals. Let's go.

What *is* a lead?

Technically speaking, a business lead is someone who is interested in the service or product you are selling. In Rent-to-Rent 2.0 this could get confusing, you're selling two very different services after all:

1. A guaranteed rent to landlords
2. Accommodation (either HMO or SA) to the general public

Right now, don't worry about tenants at all. Your number one priority is getting a property. The leads you are going to be uncovering are going to be two different kinds of customer: landlords and letting agents.

While which one you are after might change the details, there are four steps to this:

1. Finding a lead – in which your goal is to find a potential property and secure a viewing
2. Ensuring the property will work with your chosen strategy – this allows you to make sure that you're making a good investment that will work for your target client
3. Positioning your rent-to-rent offer – your goal here is to work out why the agent or landlord would benefit from your services and present the

offer in those terms, without overwhelming them

4. Negotiating and closing the deal – once you know that both the landlord and property are a good fit, you need to work with them to build a win-win agreement that benefits everyone

In Chapter 5, I'll tell you about how to source the leads themselves. This provides you with the strategies you'll need to get the contacts that you can then leverage into viewings and potential deals.

In Chapter 6, I look at what motivates landlords and agents to want rent-to-rent or what might put them off. Based on these motivators and objections, I share a proven system to help you present rent-to-rent as the win-win deal that it is.

The last thing you want is to be dealing with a property that requires a mountain of work, or a difficult landlord. In Chapter 7, I lay out how to use the viewing to make sure that the deal is actually going to work out for you. I also show you a few tricks to start uncovering some of the details and building the rapport which lets you position rent-to-rent as effectively as possible.

You've viewed the property and made a verbal offer to guarantee the landlord's rent. Now it's time to iron out the details. At the same time, we're trying to avoid overcomplicating the process and overwhelming the landlord, right? Chapter 8 shows you how to layer the negotiation process so nothing gets forgotten, while keeping things simple and easy for the landlord.

CHAPTER 5

Sourcing the leads

Finding your first property is intimidating. I know that one big question I had for myself while I was looking for my first deals was "if operating like this makes such a great profit, what's stopping the landlord from just doing it for themselves?" Ironically, this actually happened to me when I was searching for my first deal.

After countless calls and endless "no's", I had just managed to secure my first property viewing: a large victorian terrace property near the university, ideal for converting into a four-bed mini student HMO – or at least I hoped it would be. I arrived early wearing the only suit I owned, knocked on the door and waited for someone to answer.

As I waited, the nerves kicked in. I composed myself, took a deep breath and tried to act like this wasn't the first time I was doing this.

During the viewing, I awkwardly followed the curious landlord around the property: oversharing and stumbling over my words trying to explain what exactly it was I did. Like a parrot, I was just regurgitating everything I had learnt through courses – telling the landlord everything I thought he wanted to hear: "Five years guaranteed rent, all the management and maintenance, free refurb, etc."

My main criteria was "can I split this property into four rooms?" So, when the landlord asked me how I would achieve the necessary level of income to justify guaranteeing their rent, I didn't think twice. I explained exactly how I'd divide the property up and how much I'd charge per room.Schoolboy. Just like my shoes.

I went away feeling really pleased with myself. I'd smashed this meeting. I could see pound signs and was already counting the £100s of cash flow per month I'd be making from my first deal. I never heard from him again. The next time I saw the property listed online, he'd gone and done exactly what I'd suggested. What a guy – who does that!

My next near-miss was also my first "motivated landlord", John, and an experience I'll never forget. As we walked around the tired property it was clear the place needed work and John didn't have the capital to invest in the place. The carpets were stained, the walls were wood-chipped and the kitchen was disjointed: the separate oven unit wasn't even integrated into the rest of the kitchen! It wasn't great, but at this stage I was willing to take on less desirable properties just to get in the game.

This time, I was keen not to make the same mistakes and overshare. I spoke less – way less – and listened more; allowing him the space to open up to me. John was a broken man. His job was beating him up and the property was a headache. To make things worse, his wife hated how much time and money managing these properties ate up.

If anyone needed my help it was John, and he knew it. He was so taken by the idea of my offer that after only 15 mins of meeting me, he literally threw me the keys and said "Mate, it's yours now!"

Wow. I couldn't believe it. It had worked.

Hyped for my first deal, and with the paperwork seeming like nothing more than a formality, I began to show friends and family around; smug that I had done it. I even got some tradespeople over to carefully plan the refurb, not wanting to waste any time.

I will never forget what happened next.

On a Thursday night just a few days later, Lucy and I were sitting around the dining table. We were still on a high and we had planned a fancy meal to celebrate. We were drinking wine and about to tuck into a juicy ribeye, when my phone rang. It was John.

He opened straight away with "Simon, I'm sorry but I can't do it."

"Huh?" I stuttered.

"Look, you're a great guy and I love the idea… but my wife wants to go with the other agent."

My heart sank.

I had got ahead of myself, wasting time visiting the property like an idiot instead of getting the contract drafted and signed. I had been unsure of my shoddy contract and put it off too long. Now, his existing letting agent had found a family tenant instead.

Instead of our planned celebration, that night Lucy tried to console me. It felt like I was at rock bottom again, just like that day standing outside of the Co-op. There was something so cruel about thinking I had done it, to only have it stripped away at the last minute, that was hard to take. I was so tired.

I can't lie. I seriously considered quitting that night. For a moment, I thought about going back to music and just trying to graft my way through life praying for a big record that would pay enough to live well. But failure was not an option. I dug deep and carried on.

The very next morning, I picked myself up and got back out there. Honestly, I'm so grateful I did.

My next viewing was my first deal and all my earlier prep worked. The truth is I think the landlord knew deep-down knew it was my first deal, but he must have seen something in me. He decided to trust me and I worked hard to repay that. Five years on, I've guaranteed his rent ever since and I have even gone on to purchase the property. Crazy, right?

As time went by, I ended up working out how to make this process much easier. There's a whole process to master. The first is sourcing the lead itself and the second is making the perfect offer that solves the prospect's problem and lands you the deal.

Precisely how you source a deal depends on whether they are a landlord or a letting agent, as does how you interact with them regarding the deal you are offering (we will talk about that more in Chapter 6). At this point, our focus is only on finding a potential property – either through a letting agent or by contacting the landlord – and arranging to see the place.

My biggest word of advice here is to keep it simple. In the early days, I would overshare, overcomplicate and of course overwhelm any lead that would give me half a chance. As tempting as it is to try and fast-track the process, take a deep breath and just find a potential property first. I'll explain what comes after this in the next chapters – but let's take it a step at a time.

Five Strategies for Sourcing landlords

Dealing directly with landlords is simply better than going through letting agents. The main reason for this is that you don't need to deal with the middle-man and any of the resulting complications. Sometimes too many chefs really do spoil the broth.

More specifically, cutting out the agent in the middle makes your life easier in several ways:

- Communication flows better since you don't have to pass messages back and forth through the agent
- Since an agent offering management services takes a cut of the rent, you make more money when they're out of the picture
- You can use your own bespoke rental agreement and have more flexibility for negotiation compared to the restrictive agreements agents use
- The majority of landlords tend not to worry so much about the strict credit checks agents insist on, removing a common issue new rent-to-renters struggle with at the start
- When dealing with a landlord, the startup costs are often reduced. A landlord is more likely to be flexible on the first rent payments and any deposits – especially if you are improving the property for them – while letting agents will often require the deposit and rent upfront, in addition to potentially charging application and company let fees!

As you might guess, a direct-to-vendor deal with a landlord is the holy grail of Rent-to-Rent 2.0. However, a lot of rent-to-renters have difficulty getting to the landlords themselves. While everybody knows how to call up an agent, or see and follow up on a letting board outside a property, landlords are a bit more of a struggle.

When I started out, I definitely didn't know where to begin. It took a lot of trial and error, and eventually I ended up working out a collection of five strategies – both on the street and digitally – that allowed me to get directly to the landlords.

TOP TIP
Build relationships, even when the lead doesn't work out

A huge number of potential leads end up not working out or going anywhere. That doesn't mean that it was a dead end, or the time spent was wasted. Strong relationships with landlords are valuable, even if they aren't interested in working with you right now.

Whenever I get a landlord's name and number, I'll save it in my phone along with the property address. Then I will check in now and then – even if they or their property aren't a good fit for now, this could change in the future. I've also learnt landlords tend to know other landlords, so this can be a great way to build connections in the area.

STRATEGY 1
Networking

Whenever I say that my number one strategy to source landlords is networking, I feel like such a hippy. I always hate it when people go "your network is your net worth" and other cliche phrases. The thing is though, it *is* true.

It's also not as easy to do as it sounds. I'm a confident guy and a people person. However, when you are the new kid in the room, going up to people and initiating a conversation is daunting as hell. I remember sitting in those rooms thinking "I don't belong here. Everyone here has property experience and I don't have a clue what's going on."

If I am honest though, that's just imposter syndrome talking. First, in Rent-to-Rent 2.0, you *have* to study property to make it work. The average landlord or agent doesn't. Just by reading this book, you are well on your journey towards knowing more than your average agent or landlord because *you're working on it*.

Second, there is a trick to networking. Instead of walking around making pointless small talk or going right in for the big sell from the start, your goal is to get people interested and curious in you and what you do.

Why? No one likes to be sold to – particularly by a stranger. Think about it, when someone cold-calls you and starts selling something, you instantly switch off. Networking is the same. If you focus on building relationships and adding value, then people will be way more inclined to help you in return when you do ask.

Over the years I've been fortunate enough to meet a lot of super-successful people. What I've noticed is that they are always seeking to add value, not just take, take, take. What they've realised is that the more they give, the more they get in return. Since they are rich, they don't need to focus on the money, so their focus is on adding value.

This applies for you too. In your case, you have something of value to offer – a guaranteed rent and making properties stress-free for the landlord. You just need to get them interested. Luckily, you can network like a pro with 'The Three S's': Set-up, Seed, Sell.

- *Set-up.* There's nothing worse than trying to pitch something and when they show interest you have nothing tangible to present. Before you go anywhere, you need to have a set-up that gives you something you can share. In this case, you should already have this if you have been following my advice! Part 1 of this book is all about getting you set up as a professional business that knows what you are talking about.

- *Seed.* Now you have value to add, you can build interest. This isn't going to happen overnight. I find what works well is building up intrigue – for example, if someone asks you what you do, just say "I work in property." Now, everyone loves property, so when they ask more questions, you can explain a few more details about rent-to-rent and how it is working for you – *without* asking for anything in return. Done correctly, this is very powerful. In fact, you may even get contacts approaching *you* to ask how they can get involved!

- *Sell.* This isn't going to happen in your first networking event. What you should do is attend property networking events once or twice a month, for three months, and spend that time seeding interest and nothing else. Only once you've properly got everyone interested, is it time for you to go "you know that business I was talking about a while back? I've got an opening now finally – you know anybody that's got a property they're trying to let? I've got some interested clients, we could guarantee the rent for five years."

Finding networking events

When it comes to networking events, finding them is as easy as just searching "property events" on Google. As for what kind of networking events you should check out, there are several. Local networking events could be anything from general property meetups to landlord-specific meetups.

You shouldn't overlook events focused on business in general either. This could be a breakfast meetup with local business people and entrepreneurs or even virtual meetups. Generally business people are going to be doing well for themselves – they will either have property or know someone who does. If you can establish yourself as the property specialist in your group, you could do really well out of it.

The final kind of events are actually free property courses where they showcase different property strategies – and of course use these teasers to try to sell you a course in order to find out more. Rather than running to the back of the room and parting with your money, take the time to talk to the other people attending the course. It might be that you need help getting the finances and end up connecting with someone who has the money or assets, but doesn't actually have the time to manage them.

TOP TIP
Networking can happen anywhere

The thing about networking is that sometimes an opportunity can appear from the most unexpected places. You might end up being shocked by how many people that you already know who might be interested in your services.

One of my most successful mentees was a single mum working a full-time job with three kids under twelve. Desperate to change their lives, she had poured nearly £30,000 into property education with no results before she met me. Once we had got her set up correctly and given her confidence in a business she could be proud of, her existing network took off! She was literally scoring deals on the playground while dropping her kids off at school.

She'd be chatting away to the other mums and dads, questions like "so, what are you doing these days?" would come up. She would quietly seed away and build interest. In the end it turned out that one of the people was an HMO landlord – she ended up with multiple deals from her alone!

STRATEGY 2
Pounding the pavement

One of the biggest mistakes that people make is that they assume sourcing deals looks like this: Sit down at your desk, get online, hunt on online property portals, job done. The digital stuff is important, but you have to back it up with physical action. You have to get out there and literally *look*.

This is why I recommend staying close to home, within The Rent-to-Rent Radius I mentioned earlier (within at least 20 miles, ideally within five miles). If you are trying to source deals four hours away, you are going to struggle to consistently be on the ground. How can you get an idea of what's actually available in the area if you're not regularly out there and checking?

When I'm out and about, I take the time to drive through my area and keep an eye out for signs of a potential lead. These might include:

- Skips
- Obviously empty and uninhabited properties
- Open doors with builders on their way in and out
- Letting agent boards

When I see potential signs, I will try and ask around or maybe knock on the door to see if anybody is in that I can chat to. A particularly good time for this might be a weekend. When a property is empty, a landlord might spend their weekends on site trying to improve things – a great time to offer to take the stress of the property off their hands!

I actually got one of my first landlords this way. I was driving in my car when I noticed a house that was clearly deep into a refurb – builders, ladders and materials all over the place. I jumped out of the car, knocked on the door and I asked if the place was available for let, the moment the door opened. The guy who had opened the door was not the owner. Fortunately, the owner had just stepped out for 15 minutes.

I was invited to wait for the landlord to return, when he did, I started chatting with him about the project and building rapport. As he showed me around the place, it turned out that he was renovating it as an all-singing, all-dancing HMO with seven rooms that would be filled by an agency. I didn't try to sell at this point, all I did was seed the idea and make sure I got his number.

When I swung by a fortnight or so later, he was starting to get a bit annoyed. Apparently, the agency had not made any progress on filling the rooms yet. He was starting to feel the pressure. It was his first HMO, the work would be finished in just two weeks, and he had spent over £100,000 on the place – he needed it to work.

At this point, the seed I had planted started to pay off. He asked if I could come back again later when his wife would be there too. In his frustration, he'd mentioned me and what I do to his wife: she was keen to meet me so we could all discuss it further together. In the end, we agreed on a guaranteed rent for five years and I acquired control of the seven-bed property – a monthly net profit of over £1,000!

The best part was the landlord had fully furnished it, so all I had to do was add some basics, costing less than £500. I broke even within a month and have been profiting ever since... Now that's Rent-to-Rent 2.0!

Being on the ground regularly, speaking to people and following up made all the difference. That just can't happen when you're on the other side of the country or stuck to your computer screen.

STRATEGY 3

Traditional marketing

Most landlords are an older demographic from a different time. A lot of them are over the age of 55 or 60 – sometimes sourcing a lead requires you to go a bit old-school. This means that when you're marketing, a traditional approach often works better than a digital one like advertising on Instagram or TikTok (though, this never hurts!)

There are several ways of doing this:

Getting your own letting boards up

This actually is one of my biggest lead generators these days, I have around 50 to 60 up in my area right now. It helps to seed and attract interest while building brand awareness in my area.

Creating a simple brochure

I discussed this in Chapter 3, but landlords love having something they can look at in their own time and discuss over the dinner table with the other half. Websites are great for this, but don't be afraid to repurpose your website into a simple brochure that explains rent-to-rent to share with landlords – particularly those who might not be comfortable with websites.

STRATEGY 4

Sending out letters

One way that letting agents get their own leads is by sending out letters to landlords they know have a property available to let – what's stopping us from doing that too? Doing this is simple:

1. Search for landlords letting properties – using online property portals, letting boards and so on
2. Send them a simple letter explaining your services and how you can help them

What makes this a powerful method is that the previous leads are looking for people who *might* need your services. This method has a higher chance of attracting a lead since you are specifically targeting people who you *know* are actively marketing their properties for let.

Digital sourcing strategies

You will notice that most of the strategies up till now don't directly use the internet at all. This approach is more modern, making use of the internet to find and contact landlords. There are a range of different websites and platforms that you can use here, but the method is generally the same.

Like dealing with agents, less is more when trying to source a lead here. The key (as always) is to seed curiosity and build rapport before trying to sell anything.

Start the conversation with a simple "hey, your property looks great! Can I arrange a viewing?" Once they engage, you should aim to confirm the viewing – or if asked to share a little bit more detail, build their interest further with something like "We are looking for long-term lets for our companies. Would you be available for a quick phone call to discuss this?" Remember – try to avoid oversharing and complicating things from the start.

When it comes to the websites and online property portals to use, remember that your specific location matters here! Check with your local network as to what works well for your area. For me personally in my corner of the UK, I have four that I recommend:

- OpenRent
- Gumtree
- SpareRoom
- Facebook

OpenRent

This is an amazingly powerful digital tool for contacting landlords. Effectively, they are almost a kind of broker that allows a landlord to upload properties to their platform. They then share those properties on every major online property portal for a small fraction of what it would cost the landlord to do it themselves.

Using this platform, you can find landlords letting properties in your area and send them a direct message. Something to be aware of, however, is that

OpenRent has become popular in recent years – this means that it can be very cluttered, so be patient and consistent and you will find some gems

Gumtree

Gumtree has its advantages and disadvantages. The main disadvantage is that it's not really seen as a place to look for properties to let, and it's a bit of a free-for-all as a result. This means that the quality of property can be a little lower. You also have to be careful of scams such as being charged a fee to view a property that doesn't actually exist.

Its main advantage, however, is that if you are a member, some landlords will allow you to reveal their number so you can phone them directly yourself. This is really useful compared to OpenRent, in which you have to send a message through their portal and wait for the landlord to message you back.

TOP TIP
Don't ever pay for a viewing!

According to the Tenant Fees Act of 2019, there are strict limits on what a landlord or letting agent can or can't charge as fees when renting out a property. Among these is charging for viewings!

This means that if you get charged to do a viewing, it is not very likely that the property itself is legit. Paying for viewings is often a quick and easy route to getting scammed.

SpareRoom

Mentioning SpareRoom when looking for entire properties might seem strange – it's the leading marketplace for renting out rooms after all. However, it can be an amazing way of finding and getting in touch with HMO landlords.

Typically, if you see properties on SpareRoom which clearly have multiple rooms for rent at once, you may have found a motivated landlord. If you notice that the photos look fairly tired and all the rooms have been up for a while, then that might be a sign that the landlord is struggling a bit.

At this point, it might be worth contacting them and seeing if they'd be willing to rent you the entire property for a discount in exchange for the guaranteed rent.

Facebook

It is also possible to find properties on Facebook Marketplace. This can work out really well – more and more people use it as Facebook grows. It is also amazingly simple to contact and talk with people.

However, like Gumtree, it has its issues. Scams can be common, so it is vital that you make sure that you're not going to get messed around before you commit to anything or pay anyone. Lots of agents use it as well - keep in mind that it is entirely possible that any message you send is going to end up with an agent, rather than the landlord themself.

Once you have made contact with the landlord, your next step is to arrange a viewing to check the property out in person. I'll talk more about this conversation in a second. Before that, we should cover sourcing deals with letting agents.

Sourcing letting agents deals

Ultimately, it is true that dealing directly with the landlord is better in the long run. However, when sourcing leads, going through a letting agent at first can be a shortcut to your first deal.

This is mostly because letting agents are honestly the lowest hanging fruit. They are guaranteed to be already marketing their properties – sourcing a deal could be as simple as walking into their branch or seeing what properties they have available online. From there, all you need to do is arrange a viewing – a task that is not quite as easy as it sounds!

If, however, you can establish a relationship with an agency, this can be an amazing source of ongoing business for you as well. One landlord is only going to have a very limited number of properties you could manage. An agency, however, could potentially be managing thousands – if you can convince them to give you a shot, this could lead to a huge amount of business from one agency alone.

I have working relationships with letting agents that have given me over ten deals and counting. This has really helped me scale quickly. Since they know the type of properties I look for, they can hit me up immediately to give me first refusal when one becomes available. This means I get a steady stream of properties coming to me and they get to save a ton of time and energy by cutting out the need to market the property and do viewings with the public.

A win-win for everyone!

There are some downsides, however.

Sourcing leads from a letting agent when you are starting out is complicated. Nine times out of ten, they will want to do credit checks and other background checks. If you are a new business, you are going to need a personal guarantor. Without a guarantor to back you up, you might be better off coming back to deal with letting agents when you are more established.

On top of this, letting agents are often not great fans of rent-to-rent for two reasons.

First, they might see rent-to-rent as a threat. We don't just help manage the property and fill the rooms, we also offer the landlord a guaranteed monthly rent whether the properties are full or not – as well as a free cosmetic refurb! It is easy to worry that once their landlords get a taste of both having a guaranteed rent and being completely hands-free, they'll never go back to the agent.

Second, many agents don't quite get what it is and why it could be valuable. Because they don't understand it, they are scared of it. As a result, they end up getting super protective of their landlords.

The problem in both cases is with communication. If you can manage to present and sell yourself well, it can help you overcome several issues. There are two parts to this – understanding how a letting agent's business model works and understanding where their concerns come from (and, therefore, how to overcome them).

A letting agent's levels of service

Letting agents offer three different levels of service, each of which mean they have a different level of involvement and responsibility with the property. Understanding the level of service that the agent is providing the landlord can be a useful indicator of how territorial they might become about rent-to-rent – in addition to what the landlord's motivations and needs are.

Service level one
This level is on the bottom of the pyramid and is just "tenant find" only. In return for a one-off fee – typically between £500 and £1,000 – the agents will source tenants for a landlord. The agents take care of the technicalities – carrying out the reference checks and making sure all legal documents are signed and correct – and then pass the tenant on to the landlord.

In this case, the landlord would manage the property maintenance and tenants themselves. Landlords choosing this service typically like to get their hands dirty and stay involved with the property.

Service level two
At service level two, the agent stays more involved with the tenants. In addition

to offering "tenant find", the agent will also be collecting the rental income for the landlord in exchange for around five to eight per cent of the rent.

What this service does not include is maintenance, which is still the landlord's responsibility. Landlords choosing this service like to keep control of the maintenance, but don't want to be responsible for collecting or chasing outstanding rents.

Service level three

Another term for this service is "fully managed". At service level three, the landlord won't be particularly involved with the property. They have delegated everything to the letting agent, who will be finding tenants, collecting rent, and maintaining the property on an ongoing basis.

Generally, the higher the level of service that the agent is providing, the more protective they will be of the landlord. An agent only offering "tenant-find" is not going to mind particularly who the tenant is once they have successfully passed all of the checks – they get paid at the point of handover and then move onto the next client. An agent for a fully managed property, however, will be used to the recurring income – they might be concerned about the similarity between your services and that they might lose business to you.

In reality, rent-to-rent works amazingly for letting agents regardless of the level of service – even at the highest level of service, the agent can still conduct their full duty and receive their monthly commission as normal. The added benefit for the agent is that just like the landlord received "guaranteed rent", the agent would also receive "guaranteed commission" for the entire term of our agreement. Another win-win, right?

Understanding how involved in a property the agent is means that you can get where they are coming from. This means that you can communicate with them better and present rent-to-rent as an opportunity to work together – which we will talk about more in Chapter 6.

Potential concerns for letting agents

Something important to understand about letting agents is that 90 per cent of the tenancies they deal with tend to be the same. This means that they have specific predefined contracts and processes which are normally the same for all of their tenants.

Rent-to-rent, however, doesn't fall into the tidy box that they normally deal with. This means that they have to use a different agreement and their role and liabilities might change. Not only is this unfamiliar and scary to them, but it also represents more work: they have to mess around with their agreements and they might even have to get head office to sign off on everything. In comparison, a normal tenant such as a family of four might seem safer and easier for them.

The trick here is to build trust in yourself and your services by making things as simple and straightforward as possible for them.

CASE STUDY
The power of simplicity

When I first started doing rent-to-rent, the general advice was to start by calling an agent. I heard that the thing to do was to speak to them about properties to let, arrange a viewing and pitch them the idea of rent-to-rent. I'd call them up and then just get "no" after "no".

The problem was that I was saying all the wrong things and overwhelming them. I'd overshare, use the intimidating and unfamiliar term of "rent-to-rent". Even after I started trying to simplify by turning up in a suit with my informative leaflets, it was still really hard to get agents on board.

Fast forward a few months. I'd now got a more professional image and I'd managed to get a couple of direct-to-vendor deals under my belt. I started leveraging these and ended up managing to build some trust and rapport with a couple of agents. Before I knew it, I was negotiating and doing deals with these agents who had always avoided rent-to-rent like the plague before.

What stuck with me is what one said to me after I signed my first deal with her. She told me "you know what, we've never done this before. The reason we've gone with you is that you've just made it really easy."

To cut a long story short, you need to find a way to keep it simple. The moment it becomes complicated or feels like hard work, they'll just bounce.

As with landlords, once you've got a potential deal with a letting agent, the next step is a viewing.

Securing viewings

Of course, it does not matter how many of the sourcing strategies you attempt if you don't secure viewings. Viewings + Offers = Deals: it is as simple as that.

The more viewings you secure and the more offers you make, the more deals you will get. Therefore, it stands to reason that one of the most important skills in being successful in rent-to-rent is knowing how to secure viewings!

When it comes to securing the viewing, there are two approaches: direct and indirect.

The difference is basically at which stage you start presenting the offer to the landlord or agent.

The direct approach is calling or turning up in person and just laying all your cards on the table at once. You pitch your service to them and then ask if they are interested or if they are agents, whether they have any properties with landlords who might be interested. They'll then either give you a straight "yes" or "no".

The trouble with the direct approach is that you will get a lot of "no's". Its weakness is that it is a lot to dump on them at once, and you haven't had a chance to build rapport and understand their key motivators first (which I'll cover in Chapter 6).

Think about it: this might be a business, but these interactions are the first steps toward forming a relationship with them, right? Of course oversharing right from the start is going to get you a quick and embarrassing rejection! Would you ever ask someone to marry you on the first date? You'd go slow and take it one step at a time, right?

The indirect approach does the business relationship equivalent. It avoids sharing too much information too soon and overwhelming your prospect. This gives you the time to understand the deal and the other party – letting you position the offer in a way that'll appeal to the landlord or agent.

First, you make an appointment to view the property – either through arranging it with the landlord or through the agency. Then you get to interact with them and get a better picture of their situation. This means that you can then pitch your offer far more effectively, ensuring it solves their problem.

TOP TIP
Don't lie or bamboozle landlords or agents

The key to the indirect approach is that you never mislead or lie to anyone at all – you are just avoiding oversharing and making things seem too complicated or challenging. If they ask you anything that requires you to share your plans in more detail – for example, "is the property for yourself?" or "when do you intend to move in?" – be honest about your intentions for the property.

Less is often more here, but being honest is important. You are trying to build trust and rapport with them. Being dishonest or misleading them might either undermine this or lead to bigger problems down the road.

If you get a "no" when this happens, don't worry. Not every potential lead or viewing is going to turn into a deal.

Ultimately, whether you are trying to source leads through agents or landlords, remember that this is a numbers game. Not every lead is going to work out and there could be a number of different reasons why. If you keep up the momentum and keep working at it, you will eventually secure a deal that works for all parties involved. For accountability, I use a deal diary to keep a record of all my viewings. You can access my template at http://www.simonsmithonline.com/book-resources.

Now you have found your leads and secured a viewing, you're well on your way. During the viewing, there are two challenges you need to handle: understanding the agent or landlord we will be working with so we can position rent-to-rent as something they need and want, and checking the property itself will work for our chosen strategy.

YOU SHOULD HAVE	• A strategy to find local landlords who might benefit from rent-to-rent using
	  - Networking
	  - Exploring your area
	  - Traditional or digital marketing
	  - Finding the landlord's details and contact them directly
	
	• A strategy to source deals with letting agents who would be interested in working with you

CHAPTER 6

Assessing landlords and agents – uncover their motivators

Once you have got a potential lead – whether it is through an agent or direct to a landlord – and you have a secured viewing, the next step is to get them excited about working with you and the opportunity you are offering them. This is where a lot of beginner rent-to-renters mess up. They will go in for the hard sell right from the start of the viewing and focus on why they think the prospect *should* want to work with them.

Remember that Rent-to-Rent 2.0 is about running a business as a professional offering a valuable and high quality service. Rather than going on about the perceived benefits, it is far more effective to spend your time building rapport while fact-finding about the client. Once you know more about the person you are actually talking to, then you can start connecting the dots between their issues and how the benefits of rent-to-rent could actually help.

And guess what? Sometimes they won't connect the dots, rent-to-rent won't be the right fit, or they won't be suitable for us and that's just fine too. Trust me, coming away with no deal is better than a bad deal.

Paying attention to the prospect is vital here. Often, I find some rent-to-renters will focus entirely on the property by itself. The landlord is just as important – it's a 50/50 split. If the property is perfect, but the landlord is unsuitable (or vice versa), then you are going to be struggling later.

After completing hundreds of viewings, I have developed a framework to conduct the perfect viewing:

1. **The rapport.** Building rapport with the prospect: You want the owner to trust you and see you as a credible opportunity.
2. **The property.** Assess the property itself: This is the time for you to look at the property itself and see if it has the potential to be your ideal deal. You need to know what to look for, what to avoid, and develop a sense for how much any cosmetic refurbishment will cost.
3. **The motivators.** Fact-finding regarding the landlord (and letting agent, if you are working with one) and their needs: Get to know their experience with the property and find out their motivators, preferences and in some cases pain points so you are best informed to pitch your solution.
4. **The offer.** This could be the only shot you get, so always make an offer and pitch your solution to their motivations at the end of the viewing. Remember to focus on their motivations!
5. **The objections.** Pay attention to the prospect's objections: perhaps their body language changes when you talk about a long-term let or they seem uneasy trusting you as a new business. If you have been building rapport with them and paying attention, you should have an idea of where these objections are coming from. At this point, it is your job to identify if it is possible to overcome these doubts or concerns at all.

What you will notice is that very little of this framework is about you. During this process, you are not the focus or the star – don't fall into the trap of leading with an information overload about yourself and your services.

The time to talk about you will come right at the end, at which point, you will have the following going for you:

- You've built rapport with them, so they trust you.
- You know what the strengths and weaknesses of the property are.
- You can identify things you can do with the property and how much money you will need to invest and how much profit to expect.
- Finally, you know what motivators you need to be offering solutions to. This means that any pitch you make can be focused and targeted to fit their motivators and any potential objections.

We will talk about steps 4 and 5 more in Chapter 7, however, to begin with let's look at motivators.

LANDLORD CASE STUDY
How Sandy gets peace of mind

When Sandy first bought her second property to rent out years ago, it was right next to her house – managing it was painless. Since then, she needed to move across the country and she now lives three hours away. Fortunately, she's managed to get the mortgage paid off so the hassle of the occasional void isn't really something she worries about too much.

Sandy is more concerned with the property being looked after in her absence. Her last tenant ended up trashing the place completely. Fixing the damage herself has meant that she has lost her last four weekends driving the six hour round trip and spending her time at the property, rather than with her family.

Having to deal with a rent-to-renter insisting that she wants guaranteed rent and her property to give her amazingly high yields is all well and good... but it's not actually solving her pain point. Her main issue isn't the money, it's the time and effort. All she really wants is someone who will take great care of her property and treat it with respect.

Anyone looking to convince Sandy to sign a rent-to-rent deal needs to focus on the benefits that she actually wants rather than forcing their agenda. Focus on how you are extremely local to the property and will ensure everything is looked after: you do regular cleans and inspections and you will go the extra mile to ensure you find the right tenants.

For rent-to-rent to work out in the long run, it needs to be a natural fit and it should benefit all parties. The owner will know what they want and need from you already. If you nervously rush in and start firing off all the perceived benefits of rent-to-rent that you hear about online or on a one day free property course, you wont stop to listen to what's actually important to them.

This means you'll find yourself guessing and losing the deal, rather than listening and meeting their needs with confidence.

Remember, rent-to-rent is not for everyone. In such cases, it is better to respectfully move on rather than forcing the issue.

Identifying motivators

When you are looking for the reasons why a landlord or letting agent might be interested in rent-to-rent, it is easy to think of it as simply looking for problems, issues and pain points. The thing is, assuming that there *has* to be a problem might mean you miss something. Marketing your service to only the clients actively suffering means you might miss out on a huge chunk of business.

Think of Holland & Barrett. They sell health products like vitamins and so on, but they don't just target people who are actively sick. True, if you are sick, vitamins will get you feeling better faster – but what about someone who is just fine, but wants to feel even better? Or wants to stay healthy and prevent illness? Instead of targeting just the pain point, "I feel awful", they target what their customers actually want to achieve: "I want to feel great".

For this reason, I prefer to look for motivators – what a landlord or agent is trying to achieve – over just their pain points. This means I don't need to wait for a lead to actively have trouble before I can work out how they might be receptive to a rent-to-rent deal.

Landlord motivators

For most landlords, their main motivation is going to be that they want their property to run with minimal headaches and hassle. When it comes to under-standing their specific situation and what will make rent-to-rent attractive to them, it helps to know the common challenges landlords face.

Tenancy voids
The whole point of having an investment property, and one of the most common motivators for landlords, is to generate income from it. When your property is empty, that can't happen.

If a landlord can't fill a property or is having particularly long gaps between tenancies, then this will become an issue. The regular monthly payments, such as the mortgage, insurance, bills and so on, won't stop just because there are no tenants. Without the rent from the tenants, the landlord will have a burning hole in their pocket – this can get scary. This might be particularly true for accidental landlords who inherited a property and responsibility they never asked for!

Exactly why they are struggling to find tenants might vary from case to case. Perhaps the letting agent they are using isn't doing their job. It could be that the property isn't in great condition and putting tenants off, or even that they are asking for too much. This can go for whole properties, but it also applies to

HMOs. A landlord might have three out of five rooms filled and is still losing money as a result.

Fortunately, you will have done the research already – if you are looking at their property, it is safe to say that you are confident that you can help (whether this is as an HMO or SA). This means that you can make sure they don't need to worry about tenancy voids since you will be offering them a guaranteed rent while taking the job of finding tenants off their hands. If there are other jobs to be done like adding more value to the property, you can handle that too.

There might be a small "preparation period" at the start in which you and the landlord agree that you don't pay rent while refurbishing the property. Once this period is over, however, you will be paying guaranteed rent and they will not need to worry about voids for the rest of the time you both work together.

Length of tenancy agreements

Something connected to tenancy voids is the length of the tenancy agreement itself. A traditional tenancy agreement lasts for six to twelve months and then the tenant could technically move out if they wanted. This potentially means the landlord needs to go through the lengthy, expensive and annoying process of refreshing the property and finding new tenants every six months.

This void time could potentially wipe out their profit for the entire year on the property.

Rent-to-Rent 2.0 agreements, however, last a long time – typically anywhere between two to five years, ideally. You want the agreement to last as long as possible yourself to ensure that *you* are making money and getting cash flow from the property after all. This means you can promise them that they won't need to worry about the future tenant for the next few years – not just the next six months.

When the owner can't sell the property

It might be that their motivation is to actually sell the property. If they can't do that, you might end up with an accidental landlord who does not want to be managing the property, but can't afford to not let it out.

I once worked with a guy who had gotten a job down south and wanted to move closer to his new offices. However, he couldn't find a buyer and, therefore, was forced to stay in the property and commute for hours to and from work every day. In the end, we helped him refinance to the correct mortgage and took over the management of the property, providing him with an additional income.

Our ability to enable accidental landlords to be completely hands-free is really valuable. On top of this, you might have situations where you could guarantee the landlords the rent until such time as you are in a position to purchase the property from them (a purchase lease option).

For example, the landlord might be asking for 300 grand for the property. However, you know from your market research that they might only get 260 grand at best if they were to sell today. You could negotiate the option to purchase the property for the full 300 grand asking price – but only after having completed a five-year contact. This can be an extremely powerful way of scaling your owned property portfolio.

Properties getting neglected

A landlord's property is valuable to them. It's either a source of income to them or even somewhere they have an emotional connection to. They want their property to be well-maintained and cared for, even if it is just because they don't want to constantly be doing repairs or paying someone else to do it.

Tenants on the other hand don't have the same motivation. A typical tenant doesn't have as much respect for a property, particularly if they know they are only going to be there for between six months to a year. This means that they might not look after the place as much as they should. In the extreme worst cases, they might absolutely trash the property. This can add up to thousands of pounds in damages.

I've come across situations where the property was a disaster by the time the tenant left. In some cases, the tenant failed to tell the landlord that their pets had ruined brand-new carpets throughout the property. In another case, I remember talking to a landlord who was horrified to find out that a family with eight kids had left drawings all over every wall.

In rent-to-rent, however, it is absolutely in our interest to look after and maintain the landlord's property – if we don't, then we can't monetise it either!

This means that we need to be absolutely on it. We need to keep the maintenance up – try running an SA with a broken radiator, the guests will be on you in a heartbeat. We also need to provide regular cleaning inspections – tenants don't want to live with a filthy housemate and you certainly would struggle to fill an empty room when prospective tenants see a messy place during a viewing.

In Rent-to-Rent 2.0, we also want to make sure the properties we are renting are as high quality as possible. This means that we have a vested interest in not just maintaining the property, but improving and investing in it as well to make sure that it is in the optimum condition.

Rent arrears and eviction woes

It's not just difficulty filling a property that can disrupt getting a regular rent from a property. Sometimes you get tenants who just refuse to pay rent. When this happens, the solution is often more complicated than just kicking them out. In the UK, tenants have rights – evicting a tenant can get complicated quickly.

Typically the rent arrears have to have reached a certain amount and there are certain legal and court proceedings that need to be followed. No landlord wants to deal with that. Potentially spending months without rental income can lead to some very deep financial problems and pain – particularly if the landlord is counting on that income to pay their bills or pay off the mortgage.

Rent-to-Rent 2.0 makes this a non-issue for the landlord. On top of providing guaranteed rent (making rent arrears our problem, not the landlord's), we don't use a standard tenancy agreement. Technically, we aren't tenants – we are a company operating under a management agreement.

This means that in the unlikely situation that we aren't paying rent or fulfilling our other obligations, the landlord has more control and influence over what happens. We discuss break clauses and negotiating how to cancel the agreement in more detail in Chapter 8.

Being on call all the time

Besides money, two huge motivators for landlords are reclaiming their time and energy. Tenants can often be really demanding and might end up calling you at all hours of the day and night to complain. I know that I have had far too many Sunday night dinners with my wife disrupted by tenants locking themselves out, or similar nonsense.

Depending on their situation, landlords might not have the time, energy, or desire to be constantly dealing with problems. An accidental landlord might have never wanted the responsibility in the first place. A long-distance landlord might not be close enough to come over to help – they might not even be in the same time zone! A landlord looking to retire might want to step back from the responsibilities.

The difference between these landlords and you is that you want to take on the responsibility. As we discussed in Chapter 2, you can invest the money, time, and energy into making this work so you can generate the cash flow to fulfil your own goals.

Initially, you may be up for taking phone calls on a Sunday night at 8pm (even if your other half gets annoyed at you answering the phone during dinner). You know that in exchange for this annoyance, you're making more than your 45-hour-a-week job was ever able to provide for you.

What you can offer the landlord is the benefit of being entirely hands-off from managing their property. Your only goal is to run the property as well as possible while bothering them as little as possible. They only have to hear from you about problems when it is truly important.

When should you contact the landlord?

With Rent-to-Rent 2.0, you want to let the landlord be as hands-off as possible. However, there are going to be things which the landlord has to know about or deal with. There are two things you can do to make your life easier when deciding when to get the landlord involved.

The first is to set out and define exactly how, when, and why the landlord should get involved from the beginning. This typically will happen during the negotiation, which I'll talk about more in Chapter 8. This means that you – or anyone else on your team – will already have an idea of when and why to contact the landlord for most situations.

The second is that you should generally handle as much of what you can before reaching out. Typically, anything minor that might cost you £30 to £40 could be sorted without even mentioning it, for example. I personally don't set a specific price, but try to do my best without losing money.

In cases where the landlord should be responsible, such as issues with electrics, heating, plumbing or structural issues, they should know about it. However, even if they should be financially liable, I try to make things as painless as possible by arranging things for them as best I can. All they have to do is sign off on it and make sure that everything is paid for.

Landlord objections

It's not just the motivators – the reasons the landlord will want to say "yes" to you – that you need to be aware of. You also need to understand any potential objections – the reasons they might say "no".

Their rent expectations
Money is a huge motivator for landlords and it can also lead to potential objections.

A landlord is going to want the maximum amount of rent they feel their property is worth and they are going to want this sooner rather than later. Something you need to pay attention to is that their expectation is not always going to match the information they might have put out online. I have come across several situations in which a property might be listed for £1,800, but in reality the landlord's asking price is £2,000, for example.

You will have done your research, so you have two options when you find this out: pay the full asking price, or try to negotiate the rent down. If you know that £2,000 works perfectly fine for what you have planned, then the landlord will probably offer to give you the keys on the spot.

If they're being unrealistic, then they might respond with an explanation of what they expect. This is a reason why having your market research handy is always valuable since you can talk them through your maths on how much they could expect to charge. If they still don't change their mind or budge, then you should just politely move on – they are probably not going to be a good fit for you.

Length of agreement
Not every landlord will plan on holding the property forever. The length of term they are willing to consider and sign an agreement for will depend on their future intentions for the property. Understanding this is key: make sure you listen to their needs and be flexible when negotiating on the potential term.

What if you can't hold up your side of the agreement?
It is true that rent-to-rent asks landlords to show you a lot of trust that you can actually deliver what you are promising. A landlord who has been burnt before by bad agents or had their property trashed by tenants who refused to pay rent might want some reassurance.

As I have already mentioned, unlike traditional tenants, the landlord has a lot more control over the agreement and you can offer them more protection, and options, if they aren't satisfied. This gives them a lot more control over the agreement and you can offer them more protections, and options, if they aren't satisfied.

Letting agent motivators

Just like landlords, letting agents will have their own motivations for accepting a rent-to-rent deal. Generally speaking, what a letting agent gets from rent-to-rent is an easier life. Some motivators might actually be similar to a landlord's, while others might be more specific to agents.

Reducing tenant turnover

One of the primary jobs of an agent is to find tenants to occupy their properties. As with landlords, the less an agency has to find new tenants to fill a property, the easier their lives become.

Every time a tenant moves in or moves out creates additional workload for the agent such as inventories, inspections and further paperwork. On top of which, during tenancy voids, the agency is not going to be earning their monthly management commission from the rent.

What rent-to-rent offers here is effectively a letting agent's Holy Grail. We become their company let tenant for up to five years, during which time they are earning some of the easiest monthly commissions they'll ever get!

Adding value to a property

Something that every agent dreads is trying to let a property which is tired and needs work. It doesn't matter how good they are at their job, no tenant wants to live somewhere that is in bad condition. This is unfortunately a problem that the agent can't do anything about themselves – if the landlord isn't interested in investing, the agent is screwed.

On the other hand, adding value and refurbishing the property is one of the specific services we are offering. An agent who lets a property out to us can finally get rid of a property that was previously impossible to let.

Once you have built up a relationship with an agency, this could in fact be a source of additional deals for you. When the agency takes on a property that needs fixing up, they can bring you in to refurbish and manage it for them!

A ready-made repeat client

An issue with the more traditional lets is that a family or tenant only ever rents one property at a time. This means that even if the agency gets repeat business from a tenant, it's only ever going to be once a year or so at best.

Rent-to-Rent 2.0, however, isn't trying to let once every few years. We have the capacity to take on and manage several properties every month. I mean, last year, I was taking on five properties every month for the entire year! If a letting agent had been letting all of them to me, they'd have filled 60 properties off one lead alone!

This lets them just pass on a potential property directly to you. There is no need for them to market it, take photos, or hunt for tenants. Plus, they don't need to do any messing around with applications or credit checks – they already know who you are and that you are good for it.

All they need to do is pick up the phone and say "you know that property on Smith Street? We have another one five doors up, you up for it?"

Letting agent objections

Some of the most common objections I get from agents, I have already mentioned in Chapter 5:

- Our services overlap with an agent's, so they might see us as a competition and threat
- Agents aren't familiar with who we are and what we offer, they might prefer to stay with a familiar approach

Company policy
The head offices of some larger corporate letting agencies have made a blanket policy to not work with rent-to-renters, simply to remove any potential liability and ensure they take as much control of their properties and tenants as possible.

This means it doesn't matter what you do, how hard you sell, or how much the local agent likes you – they have to follow company policy and, therefore, you're probably wasting your time. Make a note this agent is a no-go and move on...

Not seeming a threat
It is easy for an agent to see rent-to-rent as a threat. They might see you as the ultimate solution and be scared that a landlord might choose to work with you directly instead. The key is to help position things so that they understand that you are offering them a mutually beneficial partnership if you work together.

The cardinal sin that rent-to-renters make with letting agencies is, ironically, using the term "rent-to-rent". This is a term which is going to be unfamiliar to them – they won't understand it and they might look down on it. So, what would be a more comfortable way for us to describe ourselves that they'll understand more easily?

Imagine: If Amazon sent five executives to the UK for six months, what would they do for accommodation? A serviced accommodation or a hotel room would get too expensive very quickly. What they would do instead is contact a letting agent and find their executives temporary accommodation as a company.

So, you have a company and business entity that is looking to let a property as a company in order to provide accommodation to tenants that they will deal with themselves. The letting agency doesn't need to worry about the tenants and the company will take responsibility for the property. Sound familiar?

Aligning yourself with local companies that have an abundance of clients that you will be providing accommodation for is a far more familiar situation to an agent. You can then let them know that you are able to guarantee the property's rent on a long-term basis, giving everyone what they want.

Often, they will have understandable doubts and concerns about this. They might worry that:

- As a brand-new company, you won't be able to pass their checks
- They might want more direct control to look after their client, the landlord
- They might have heard horror stories about "traditional" rent-to-renters who tried and failed – ending up with complaints and failures to pay their rent

The key here is to build a relationship and trust with them.

Doing this means you need to focus on getting individuals on board, rather than trying to sell the entire company on rent-to-rent at once. This is how I do it. I network with key people who are influential in the agency. They can then champion the business, and concept, internally for me and we can build up from there.

I remember starting off with one guy. By developing a relationship and rapport with him, he was able to build me up within his agency. Eventually, I found myself sitting down with the director of the agency, which ran around 3,500 properties in the local area alone. We were able to broker a deal in which they would pass me an abundance of properties in the area.

Getting one agent on your side can make your entire business, even though it is harder.

What next?

Positioning rent-to-rent isn't something that happens in the first five minutes of talking to an agent or landlord or a viewing. Getting this done right takes time – sometimes it takes a while for a sceptical landlord or agent to come around!

The key is that you can't force it. A "no" today doesn't always mean "no" tomorrow, so stay patient and never burn your bridges. Rent-to-rent works best when working together!

This means that a lot of the advice from this chapter is going to be useful while dealing with landlords and agents in general. Remember to always keep your eyes open for motivators and potential objections – how are they telling you that they will benefit from rent-to-rent?

YOU SHOULD HAVE	• An awareness of what motivates the landlords and agents you are interacting with • A plan for countering any possible objections

CHAPTER 7

Assessing the property – Is it a valuable investment?

Apart from being your best opportunity to understand the agent or landlord's motivators and objections, as well as build rapport, the viewing is your first opportunity to see the property itself. At this point, you need to assess the property itself to see if it can work with your chosen strategy – then present a well-positioned verbal offer by the end, if it is right.

General approach to the viewing

Your communication during the viewing needs to be two things: complimentary and curious. While being friendly and nice about the property, you want to be subtly digging and asking questions and making mental notes to support your understanding of their motivators and potential objections.

A useful trick to simultaneously get a lot of information while building rapport is to clarify your understanding by repeating or summarising what you have just learnt. This gives them the opportunity to correct anything you might have misunderstood while also demonstrating that you are paying attention to what is going on.

Another thing to remember is that using open question terms like "who", "what", "how", or "why" will give the prospect the opportunity to share more detail. A closed question like "Do you…?" or "Can you…?", on the other hand, is much easier to answer with just "yes" or "no" – forcing you to push harder for more information.

Here are examples of questions you can ask prospects to help you on your way:

LANDLORD	AGENT
What's the story with this property?	Do you know the Landlord? What's their situation?
What kind of tenants did you have before? How were they?	Is the Landlord planning any works to the property before it will be ready?
Do you manage the property yourself? If so, do you enjoy it?	When is it available from?
If not, which agent do you use? How has your experience with them been? What could they do better?	How long has the property been on the market?
Do you plan on doing any works to the property?	Does the landlord live in the local area?
Do you have all your safety certificates in place?	What do you think of this property? Is it your first time here also?
How long has the property been on the market?	Have you had much interest? Any offers yet?
When is the property available from?	What is the landlord looking for?
How long has the property been vacant for?	Do you know if they would be interested in a long-term let?
How long have you owned the property?	Do you fully manage the property or just assist the landlord with tenant finding?
What are your long-term plans for the property?	If yes, how long have you been managing the property for?
Do you have a mortgage on the property?	Do you think the landlord has a mortgage?

An example of this kind of fact finding while building rapport might look like this:

You: "Do you manage the property yourself?"

Landlord: "Yes."

You: "How is that going for you?"

Landlord: "Well, it was fine ten years ago… but now I'm getting on a bit. I've got other commitments, I have grandchildren… I don't want to spend all of my free time dealing with the tenants."

You: "What do you mean by all your time?"

Landlord: "Well, lately it feels like between this place and my other properties I'm spending all my weekends here instead of with the family."

You: "Yeah, sounds like a lot… what else is going on?"

Landlord: "Hmm…. on top of that, it's becoming hard to let the property because it could do with some work doing to it, like new carpets.. The thing is, I can't afford them right now if I'm honest."

You: "So… what you're saying is that ten years ago, you had the time to do this. Now you have the grandchildren, you have less time and you would prefer to spend your weekends with them. This means you're not finding the tenants as easily. Also, you recognise some work needs doing, but don't currently have a budget for this. Is that right? Is that fair?"

If you have summarised the information incorrectly or misunderstood something, the owner will usually turn around immediately and tell you so. On the other hand, if you get it right, they'll agree and you can move on.

Keep this up throughout the viewing. By the end, you should have formed a rapport with the owner and developed a better understanding of the situation – including their specific motivators and potential objections. This will allow you to target and position your initial offer more effectively at the end.

TOP TIP
Ask about their plans before sharing yours

While you are viewing the property, you might be slowly forming a to-do list for your planned refurb. However, the landlord probably is already aware of what needs to be done.

Give them a chance to share what they are intending to do before someone else moves in, before sharing your refurb plans. There is nothing worse than putting yourself on the line for buying or investing in the property if the landlord was going to do it for you until you said something!

Things to look out for

Generally, I divide the things I keep an eye out for into three categories:

- Cosmetic details
- The essentials
- Things that demand ongoing maintenance

Cosmetics include the general condition and appearance of the property, things like the carpets, radiators, skirting boards, walls and so on. Things to be careful of are things that might be more complicated to freshen up and replace – a bathroom covered from top to bottom in avocado-coloured tiles from the 60s will be a more substantial investment for you to refurbish – remember no new bathrooms or kitchens!

The essentials cover the plumbing, heating, electrics, smoke alarms and elements like windows, ventilation, or damp. Issues here can quickly become expensive and lead to frustrated and angry tenants or guests – better to get them dealt with early doors.

Particularly older properties might need a lot more specific care and maintenance to keep in good condition – for Rent-to-Rent 2.0, keep this in mind so we can optimise our time. This could include the large garden or grounds – keeping these in good condition might require hiring a gardener specifically and quickly get unsustainable – or various quirks of an old building such as rickety stairs or fragile floorboards.

If you do notice any particular issues during the viewing – particularly with maintenance or the essentials – asking what the landlord intends to do about them is important. If the landlord is not willing to address the issue – either by taking care of it themselves or accounting for them in negotiations – this might be a sign to move onto the next viewing.

TOP TIP
Get a video

There is a lot to take in on a viewing, plus you might end up finding yourself doing several viewings back-to-back. Taking a quick video of the property on a smartphone is an invaluable trick to make sure your memory stays fresh.

Once you have viewed a property and you are interested in the property and working with the owner, ask permission to take a quick five-minute video of the property. Most owners will have no issue with this, especially if they are excited to work with you. However, this might be slightly awkward if the current tenants haven't vacated the property yet – in which case, getting a video may not be appropriate.

Having this to refer to allows you to refresh your memory of anything important and gives you a second chance to notice anything you might have overlooked.

Assessing the property and potential costs

The quality of the property itself is important. Rent-to-Rent 2.0 is about providing a high quality rental to tenants or guests – if the property needs an extensive refurb, then the costs are going to add up quickly and the property may be unsuitable (unless the landlord offers to invest in the improvements required). During the viewing, you need to be continually assessing the condition of the property and what work might be needed to get it up to scratch.

My approach – which we will talk about more in the following chapters – is that we don't usually want to commit to projects beyond cosmetic refurb and furnishing the property. At the end of the day, what you need to remember is that this is not your property. The truly expensive projects – such as doing up the kitchen and bathroom – are the landlord's responsibility, not yours. Personally, I'm not in the business of investing heavily in property I don't own!

If the property is in decent condition and the bathroom and kitchen are good, anything else is straightforward. Cosmetic projects have a lot of bang for your buck – they don't cost much, but they go a long way. Painting and decorating a property might cost £1,500, putting in new carpets could cost around another £1,500. However, this investment of only £3,000 would have the place feeling brand new and you could get your initial investment out in just a few months – ideal, right?

How much should you invest?

Before you go to the viewing, you need to have worked out your estimated cash flow – the difference between what you plan to offer to the landlord as guaranteed rent plus the bills and what you estimate you'll get from tenants or guests each month.

Any investment you make into the property is something you're going to have to recoup over time. The more you invest, the longer it will take to start profiting and establishing cash flow.

My goal is to have broken even and started making a profit, within six months at most. If it takes longer than that, you are starting to ask for trouble!

For instance, if you expect to get £1,000 a month from a property, then your absolute maximum refurb budget has to be £6,000 – not a penny more!

If the property requires a greater investment than that – perhaps because the landlord doesn't have the money to invest – then you should make sure the negotiations involve how you're going to make that money back. This might involve discussing clauses like reductions to the guaranteed rent or the landlord committing to a longer term– guaranteeing that you make your money back.

Remember, however, that the viewing is not the time to go into detail on this. This will be done in a structured and layered way as you discuss the offer and negotiate the contract.

TOP TIP
Two types of investment

When calculating costs and investments, I've realised that there are two types of investment in rent-to-rent: property investments and company assets.

Property investments
Changes to the property itself, such as carpets, painting, or fitting blinds, is money that you are never going to get back. They directly benefit the land-lord because they are improvements to the property that can't be removed and taken with you once your contract is up. When calculating costs, you need to make sure you've earnt 100 per cent of your property investments back before the end of six months.

Company assets
Furnishing a property is a very different kind of investment on the other hand. When you end a rent-to-rent deal, these are all things which you could easily take with you and use in the next place or sell to recoup any investment. As a result, when calculating my break even point I generally account for 50 per cent of these costs in my calculations.

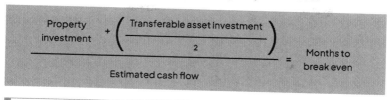

$$\frac{\text{Property investment} + \left(\dfrac{\text{Transferable asset investment}}{2}\right)}{\text{Estimated cash flow}} = \text{Months to break even}$$

CASE STUDY
How Reena dodged an expensive bullet

Reena is looking for her first rent-to-rent and has managed to get two viewings back-to-back. She estimates that the first property she sees has an estimated cash flow of £1,000 per month; the second looks promising with a potential cash flow of £1,150 per month.

As she looks around the first property, she keeps her eyes open for any refurb work that would be needed. While there is nothing major, she can tell that it has been years since it was last redecorated – the carpets and wallpaper definitely need to be changed! She also wants to make sure that the furniture is updated.

In total, she estimates that the cosmetic refurb will cost around £3,000 and furnishings will cost a further £3,000.

The second property is a little bigger with more rooms, but is in slightly worse condition. Particularly concerning is the tired kitchen that would need replacing, and the landlord doesn't have the budget. Reena estimates that refurbishment might cost £7,000 (while crossing her fingers that refurbing the kitchen isn't biting off more than she can chew) and furnishing the bigger property might cost £5,000.

	Estimated cash flow	Property investment	Company asset investment	Total to recoup	Months to break even
Property 1	£1,000	£3,000	£1,500	£4,500	4.5
Property 2	£1,150	£7,000	£2,500	£9,250	8

After doing the maths, Reena has come to a conclusion. While the second property could provide more cash flow in the long run, the increased investment costs count against it heavily. While she isn't going to give up yet – she might be able to make the second place work after some negotiation – the first property is currently a far better deal for her.

By this point, you should have a fairly good idea of if this property is going to be a good deal and if the landlord or agent will be good to work with. They should also understand what exactly you are offering them and what you intend to do with the property.

Your services should be positioned in terms of a solution that addresses the motivators of the agent or landlord. If the agent is looking for several painless lets to earn their commission, let them know that you'd be happy to take on whatever else they have. If the landlord expresses concern about late payments, poor property management, or demands on their limited time, make it clear how your solution addresses that issue for them!

For example, if you identified that the landlord's motivators were to reduce the amount of time and energy that they were investing into managing the property, you might say something like:

"So, you said that you're struggling with the management of this place. Well, we have an internal team and we can deal with it all for you. In fact, if you would prefer, we don't need to bother you for any minor repairs less than £100! We have an amazing local power team on hand to ensure your property and the tenants are taken care of so that you can sit back and relax. Does that sound good to you?"

Even if you do this all perfectly, you won't get a result every time. The statistic to remember here is that getting one deal might require you to do about ten or so viewings on average. Your earlier deals might require more patience while you are learning the ropes. Once you master the skills involved, this will improve a lot – I find I convert *at least* one viewing out of every three into a deal these days.

By the end of a successful viewing, say "yes" and make a verbal offer to take over management of the property and guarantee the landlord's rent (see Chapter 6 for advice on positioning the offer and its benefits). This should buy you some breathing space while they hold the property for you.

There are four steps to making a verbal offer:

- Say "yes", you would love to let the property
- Confirming the rent that you would be guaranteeing for them
- Agreeing on the term that you will be renting for – the longer, the better (more on this next chapter!)
- Letting them know when they can expect a written offer and – if you have not already – checking if you can take a video of the property

Part two: Sourcing and closing the perfect deal

Now, time is of the essence! Sit down to do your final due diligence and get the formal offer to them asap so you can close the deal!

YOU SHOULD HAVE	• An assessment of the property – including a plan and budget for any refurb work • An assessment of the landlord or agent – do you have a better idea of their motivators and potential objections • A simple walk-through video of the property to refresh your memory later • A verbal agreement with the owner if the property promises to be a good fit

CHAPTER 8

Making an irresistible offer

To quickly recap. At this point, you have just come back from viewing the property. What you ideally have following the viewing are:

- Videos and photos of the property on your smartphone.
- A better picture of who the prospect is – what their motivators are and any possible objections they might have to your offer.
- More clarity on how much rent would be accepted.
- An idea of the preferred length of agreement or commitment.

Based on your first impressions, you think that the property fits your needs and that you can have a positive working relationship with the landlord or agency you would be renting from. As a result, you've expressed interest in the property and given them a verbal offer.

From now on, the clock is ticking and speed is everything. The landlord or agent may have decided to take the property off the market, excited about the opportunity to enjoy a guaranteed rent and less hassle managing their property. In many cases, however, they will continue marketing the property – therefore, we can't afford to waste time. You want to make sure that you have the deal closed quickly before someone else makes an offer and grabs the property from under you.

That said, you don't want to start hurrying either and make mistakes because you got over excited about closing the deal. If you go too fast, it is easy to either confuse your offer – overwhelming the prospect and making them pull out – or to end up committing to a deal for the sake of it which does not actually suit you.

Over the years I have perfected the art of negotiating and closing rent-to-rent deals, I have worked out a winning formula that works every time. This is a layered, step-by-step approach which ensures you end up with a deal that benefits everyone involved.

Double-check everything

The first thing to do is to review all of the information that you collected throughout the viewing. During the viewing – particularly the first few times you do them – you might not have the time to fully consider every important detail. Before you commit to anything, it is helpful to go over the property and make sure that you have not missed anything important.

Some things you want to consider:

- Your photos and videos of the property: Checking this footage lets you refresh your memory of the property (particularly useful if you viewed several in a row). It also gives you a chance to reassess the quality of the property and furnishings – helping you estimate how much work needs to be done to refurbish.
- Your market research: Now you have seen the property in person, double-check that it should work for the type of clients you expected. It might be that it could be more appropriate for a different target client avatar, or what you expected to work well as an HMO might be a perfect fit for an SA (or vice versa!).
- The figures and your budget: Before you saw the property, you will have calculated how much you expected you could charge tenants. Take a second to make sure that your maths is still correct now that you know how much the owner wants to charge and for how long.

Understanding the numbers

It is vital that you understand the numbers before you start any final negotiations, and that you have them available and ready while talking with the owner. While discussing the agreement, you want to position yourself as someone professional, confident and prepared.

Being able to justify and explain the reasoning behind your requests with precise data and figures is a powerful way to convince the owner that you know what you are doing, and that they can trust you with their property. Understanding your margins also gives you the ability to be more flexible if needed.

TOP TIP
Get a second opinion

Before making any big decisions, ask someone else who knows what they are talking about, for their take. It could be that you slightly miscalculated the nightly rate, which then messes up all your figures. Perhap due to inexperience with refurbs, you underestimate the true cost of the cosmetic refurb – pushing your break-even point beyond the six month limit.

Having someone in your network – either a mentor, a coach, or from being part of a community – to double-check your deals can save you from making costly mistakes.

STEP 2
Make the offer in writing

Once you have confirmed that the property will work for you, it is time to make your official offer. Keep this stage simple – we don't want to overwhelm the owner with detail yet. Negotiation over the fine print and precise details can wait until later.

The first email only needs to reinforce the verbal offer made at the property with just the proposed rent and length of the agreement. I recommend using a structure like this:

Dear (*landlord's/agent's name*),

Thanks so much for showing me around your property.

We would love to offer you (*proposed rent*) for a term of (*duration of agreement*).

We look forward to hearing from you,

- - - - - - - - - - - - - - -

At this point, what you are waiting for is confirmation that they have accepted your offer – ideally in writing. If your offer was agreed in principle, verbally during, the viewing this will be a formality. On the other hand, this is their opportunity to formally accept the offer and take the property off the market if they had needed to go away and think about it first. Once you have their acceptance in writing, this gives you the opportunity to move on to the next level of negotiation.

TOP TIP
Don't delay in sending the offer in writing!

Keeping the momentum going here is important. Since the landlord or agent is probably going to continue doing viewings, someone else might put in an offer if you wait too long.

I recommend sending this email the same day as the viewing, just a few hours afterwards at most. If the viewing is conducted in the evening, make sure the email is sent as a priority first thing on the morning after.

STEP 3

Establish important dates and any works required

Renting out high quality properties means that you may need to carry out some work beforehand. Once you start renting a property out, you are going to want to avoid having it empty for long periods of time without tenants. This means that the first few weeks will be the best opportunity you get to make any improvements or changes.

Getting this done right from the start has several benefits:

- You have the chance to make sure that the property is in a good condition making it more attractive as a high-quality investment
- It demonstrates to the owner that you are committed to maintaining and managing the property correctly
- A refurbished property allows you to take professional photos for marketing purposes that show it at its full potential, making it easier to find tenants

- It's far easier to carry out work while the property is empty – later on, you're likely to have to work around bookings and tenancies

In Chapter 9, I walk you through the process of refurbishing a property. I recommend that at this point – before you get the keys and are still negotiating – you make a list of the work that needs to be done before the property will be ready to rent out to clients. From this list, you can create a timeline estimating how long it will take before you can start filling the place.

The ideal scenario here is for us to negotiate a rent-free period in which we do not pay rent while refurbishing the property. The key here is to position it as a 'preparation period'. Nobody likes to give something for nothing – making it clear that you will be investing in *their* property will make this step of negotiation easier.

Typically, I would advise that two weeks is good in situations where not much work is required. This might include repainting, furnishing the property, transferring the utilities and updating landlord safety certifications. A high-quality property that is already in great condition might not need a preparation period at all. Other properties might require more time to refurbish.

The duration of the agreement is important here as well. The longer you have the property for, the more time you have to recoup any investment costs. This means that not being able to secure a preparation period for a five-year agreement is less of an issue than for a shorter contract. If you are having trouble negotiating a preparation period, consider negotiating a longer term instead – allowing you to recover the investment in the long term.

TOP TIP
Discuss investments and improvements with the owner:

In a more traditional rental, the owner would usually do cosmetic works between tenancies. During the viewing and negotiations, discover what changes they had already intended to make to the property. If a normal tenant could expect a landlord to do something to a property before moving in, it is not unreasonable for you to ask for it to be done as well.

Typically, the work that you should be funding or carrying out should be a matter of taste and making sure that the property is perfect. Major works – including changes to kitchens and bathrooms – or repairs should be the responsibility of the owner, not you.

If there is work that needs to be done, but the owner does not have the

> funds to do it, you can consider using this as a solution for the negotiation. For example, asking for a longer rent-free period or agreeing on a reduced rent for the first 12 months equal to your investment level in exchange for carrying out work the owner is unable to fund.

At this stage of the discussion, you can establish (for example):

- The owner needs to replace a door and install a new washing machine
- You need to change the carpets, paint and install new blinds
- The combined time of the works would take four weeks

From this, you can agree that the first four weeks from you receiving the keys should be classed as a preparation period. Once the preparation period has passed, the first rental payment will be due.

At the end of this stage, you should have agreed on two key dates which should be on the final agreement:

- *Effective date.* This is the date you get the keys and become liable for the property. This is important because it establishes the key date at which you are in control of the property. It also protects you as the agreement begins *before* you start investing in the property. Never begin spending money on a property without a signed agreement first!
- *First payment date.* This is when your first rent payment is due. By this point, you ideally want to have the property ready and your first tenants in place. Getting this right means you could have generated the income to pay the first rent from new clients already, meaning you're not out of pocket!

> Andrew has discovered a promising property and is negotiating the details with the landlord, Mary. Having discussed the work that needs doing, Andrew and Mary have agreed that the first two weeks will be a rent-free preparation period.
>
> Currently, the property is occupied by a tenant, who will be moving out on the 15th of March. Andrew does not want to be liable for the tenant or the property until he actually has the property. The landlord has requested two days to turn the property around so his effective date is the 17th of March.

According to the terms of the agreement, Andrew's first rent payment is due on the 31st of March. By this time, Andrew needs to have refurbished the property, got it photographed, and found clients to fill the property. This means that on the 31st, he will be ready to hit the ground running and start generating cash flow.

STEP 4

Negotiate additional clauses

Once you have an agreement on the refurb and the important dates of the agreement, it is time to discuss any other clauses that you or the owner want to be included. This is an important step, as it ensures that there is no room for doubt and all relevant terms and conditions are in writing.

TOP TIP
Get legal advice

As mentioned back in Chapter 3, while you might not need to have your solicitor help you with the negotiation itself, having a lawyer helps make sure that the agreement is legally correct and binding. I have a standard template for contracts which was written up by my solicitor.

Running any legal agreements past your lawyer, particularly for your first agreements, will help protect you from any unforeseen issues.

These specific clauses might vary depending on the property and whether the agreement is directly with the landlord or you are doing the deal through a letting agent. Some typical clauses that you might expect from the owner might include:

- Rent increases during the term of the agreement – can the rental price increase, how you will be advised of any changes and how much can the rent increase by
- Landlord's access to the property – what notice the landlord must give to enter the property during the agreement and how will you be informed
- Storage of property and furnishings – If the landlord has personal

belongings in the property (perhaps as they are living abroad), how should this property be stored

I recommend that you have several "non-negotiable" clauses in the agreement by default that help ensure that the contract protects you. It is important to remember that this is not a one-sided process, however.

The aim here is to negotiate an agreement which is a win-win. This means that I aim to never give something up without getting something in return – negotiating a preparation period in exchange for investing in and refurbishing the property for example. It also means that I should not expect the owner to give something up without me giving them something in return.

Termination clause

It is hard to predict the future. If you have committed to guaranteeing a landlord's rent for five years, you want to have a clause that protects you if your situation changes during the term.

For this reason, I recommend including a two-month termination clause in the agreement. This means that if the property is not working for you, you do not end up trapped in the contract indefinitely. This can be extremely costly: I have seen people lose a lot of money due to not having this clause included in their contract.

Why might a property not work out?

There might be many reasons why you might need to use a termination clause.

1. The property ends up being unsustainable for your chosen strategy – you might struggle with filling rooms or you discover the demand for serviced accommodation wasn't what you were hoping for.
2. Unforeseen emergencies – In the event of a disaster, on a global scale such as COVID or a personal accident or illness, you might not have the ability to support the property.
3. A change in priorities – You might realise that your motivators have changed entirely and rent-to-rent is just not for you, instead you might want to move to the Caribbean and become a diving instructor!

Typically, this clause will require you to get them on board first – the owner might not appreciate the paradox of a guaranteed rent which could be cancelled at any time. The compromise that my solicitor and I drafted – which works well – is that I can give two months notice at any time for any reason, in return, the owner can give immediate notice to me if I fail to fulfil any key responsibilities.

This means that both parties are protected if they realise that the deal no longer works for them.

Assign responsibilities

Just like a traditional tenancy agreement, there are certain responsibilities that the owner would be expected to take care of. This includes: general repairs, plumbing and ensuring that both electrical installations are all fully functioning and (of course) all health and safety standards are met. Make sure that your agreement clarifies that this is the owner's responsibility.

Typically, this is not a controversial clause to include – most owners would expect this. However, it is sensible to make sure that this is explicitly stated. In return, you may decide to take care of minor maintenance issues – often capped by a monetary threshold, i.e. any repairs up to £75, you would take care of in good faith.

Another essential responsibility of the landlord is to have the necessary insurance. HMOs and SAs are generally not covered on a standard landlord insurance policy. Furthermore, some will specify no subletting and will only be valid if an AST is used with all tenants. Therefore, it's important to be transparent about your intentions for the property and ensure the landlord has the correct insurance in place.

If operating SA, it can be wise for you to get a top-up insurance policy that insures your furniture etc... Once again, please speak with a specialist insurance broker to get qualified advice.

Length of the agreement

The length of the term should have already been discussed and agreed, however, at this point you could discuss any finer details. It might be that the owner wants the option to break the agreement at the halfway point and, therefore, the appropriate break clauses may need adding to the agreement to finalise the deal.

Understanding the numbers is important here. You want to make sure that any such break clauses do not end up meaning that you have lost money on a property. Generally, my advice is to push for longer agreements where possible, increasing the chance of you earning a return on your investment – you should never approve a break clause which could impact the profitability of the deal too significantly.

Andrew is continuing his negotiation with Mary. Mary has requested that Andrew include a break clause allowing her to leave the contract at the end of the first six months if she wishes to.

Andrew knows that the property will require a £6,000 investment and expects that he will make roughly £1,000 per month.

This means that if Mary breaks the agreement at six months, his best-case scenario is to break even. Andrew wants to make sure that Mary can have her break clause, however, he also needs a return on his investment.

His solution is to offer Mary a five-year contract with a break clause at the end of a year and a half. This allows him the opportunity to get a return on his investment, while still allowing Mary to break the contract if she is unsatisfied after a year and a half.

If the owner is unwilling to negotiate a longer agreement, an alternative is to negotiate a fee for invoking the break clause early. This means in order to break the contract before you have had a chance to make a return on your investment, the owner has to repay a sum of money towards repaying you – protecting you from making a loss.

For your first deal you will need to source a trusted agreement to use or instruct a specialist solicitor to draft a suitable contract! It is important to get this right, so make sure that you have the correct paperwork that is specifically designed for rent-to-rent. The investment in an expert to draft a reusable agreement is well worth the money.

Over the years, I have invested thousands in solicitor fees to create and fine-tune my agreements based on the feedback of landlords and my experience seeing rent-to-rent deals through to the end of the term. I know how costly this can be and how hard it is to find solicitors that truly understand the model and, therefore, make my templates available for a fraction of the cost at http://www.simonsmithonline.com/book-resources.

Part two: Sourcing and closing the perfect deal

For your first deals, I recommend that you have someone check the agreement before it is officially sent to the owner. This might be by a mentor or your solicitor, and ensures that nothing important has been overlooked.

Once the contract has been finalised, send it to the owner to sign. For the sake of speed and convenience, I recommend using electronic software that allows the owner to sign with an e-signature for this.

Negotiating with landlords

Both the viewing and negotiation are important opportunities to assess the landlord and make sure that they are a right fit. In my experience, it is often the landlord (not the property) which makes the difference between a deal being a good investment or not working out. When negotiating, keep an eye out for red flags that could warn you that a landlord might be particularly challenging to deal with.

For this reason, I recommend that steps 3 and 4 in the negotiation happen as a phone call rather than through emailing. This means that you can use the conversation to feel out any possible objections – letting you offer reasonable concessions to make them more comfortable before their concern becomes an issue – and get a sense of how they are reacting to the negotiation.

By the time you are negotiating with a landlord, they have already expressed interest in your services. Typically, they will be looking for ways to make the opportunity you are offering them, work.

If the landlord is pushing back over £200 or the start date in the negotiation, they might be far more difficult once the contract has started. The last thing you want is a landlord who is resisting replacing a broken boiler in the middle of winter while you have freezing guests complaining and demanding refunds!

Always follow your gut. If you feel like you and the landlord are clashing, the landlord possibly would prefer to go it alone, or perhaps they don't seem to appreciate the value you are bringing to the table, cut your losses and walk away from the deal. I promise you, a bad deal is worse than no deal at all!

This process gets easier with time and practice. The key is to approach it with a professional mindset that inspires confidence that you know what you are doing and can provide value to the landlord.

Negotiating with agents

When dealing with letting agents, the process is slightly different to landlords. First, an agent is a middleman – acting on behalf of the landlord and, therefore, *not* the key decision maker. Second, they will have their own set processes to follow – this means you need to pass their application processes, which can be more complicated.

Once you have sent your offer to the agent – who will then pass it onto the landlord to accept – the application process begins.

1. You will receive an application form to fill out and often be asked to pay a holding fee.
2. They will run a number of referencing, affordability and credit checks on you and your company.
3. Providing you are approved, they should send you their own company let agreement.
4. You will discuss their agreement, which will need the appropriate clauses removed or modified, and lastly you will aim to get your non-negotiable clauses included.

TOP TIP
Be careful with an agency's standard agreements!

When negotiating with a letting agent, beware of any other agreements sent over to you at this stage – especially an Assured Shorthold Tenancy (AST). This is not the correct agreement for rent-to-rent and will mean you are illegally subletting – we don't want that!

There are several things to be aware of about this application process.

The holding – or company let – fee

Once you have paid the holding fee, the agent will take the property off the market while beginning the application process. However, if you fail any of the checks, you are at risk of this money not being refunded.

Make sure to check for the small print before making the payment and budget for this – including it in your operating costs when dealing with letting agents. Don't stress about this fee – it's a small price to pay and worth the risk to take for the potential of cash flowing a property for 5 years!

The checks

As a new company, you are unfortunately not going to pass the checks and referencing on your company's credit alone. This means that early on in your journey, you will need a personal guarantee or guarantor if you want to pass a credit check – either yourself or someone else.

To be a guarantor, you need to demonstrate an annual income between 30x and 36x the value of the monthly rent. This means that a rent of £1,000 requires you to make between £30,000 to £36,000 per annum.

If you do not have this income, you are going to need either a willing friend or family member who does meet the requirements to be your guarantor or something more drastic like paying six months rent upfront. If you are unable to do this, I recommend you focus on dealing with landlords over letting agents to begin with.

Close the deal and collect the keys

Closing the deal is a process which takes time, the worst thing to do is rush it. However, it is important to not waste too much time – if negotiations take too long, the owner might move onto a simpler deal.

Generally, the rule of thumb is to expect one to two weeks for this process – though this might vary. Remember that you are promising to guarantee the landlord's rent – if you make a mistake here, it could be expensive. Do not be afraid to take your time to make sure everything is done right.

Once you have sent off the agreement and it has been signed, you can collect the keys. At this point, things get real.

The clock is now ticking until the first rent payment is due and you're officially guaranteeing the landlords rent. The last thing you need is to have this property burning a hole in your wallet. If required, you need to get started with refurbishing the property and making sure that you are generating the cash flow you need to make a profit on your investment.

This is a process for which you need a systematic and optimised approach. Delays or issues at this point can become expensive and you need to make sure that everything has been done right the first time. In Chapter 9, we will look at my structured approach to making sure the refurb makes the best use of your time and resources.

YOU SHOULD HAVE

- A double-check or confirmation that the deal works
- A written acceptance of the offer
- Clearly-defined dates including – when the agreement was signed, when the agreement will take effect, when the first rent payment is due
- A professional rent-to-rent agreement for direct-to-landlord deals
- An understanding of the letting agent deal process including application process and correct agreement
- Negotiated additional details including:
  - The length of the agreement
  - Termination clauses
  - Defined responsibilities for you and the landlord

PART THREE

Securing cash flow

Part three: Securing cash flow

Once you have closed the deal and have the keys, the next step is to refurb the property and start to secure your cash flow.

As part of developing Rent-to-Rent 2.0, I have worked out frameworks for this. These guides work no matter how much experience you have – they are how I approach the refurb and filling the properties.

Each framework is based on several core principles that help make it a positive experience for the landlord and protect you from getting in over your head:

- *Have a structured and clear approach.* Trying to do everything at once is only ever going to blow up in your face. In Part 1, I explained how it was important to get all your planning and preparation done before you even think about approaching landlords and letting agents.

    It's the same here. Each framework has a specific order of events which makes sure that everything gets done in the right sequence and nothing gets forgotten. I recommend following step-by-step in order to prevent unpleasant surprises or costly mistakes.
- *Work with the landlord.* If the landlord is a good fit, they will want this to work. This is a team effort. There will be works that are the landlord's job to take care of. This means that you have to make sure that both sides are on the same page regarding who is responsible for what!

    On the other hand, as I explained in Chapter 6, your main motivation is to make the landlord's life as straightforward as possible. This means that it's a good idea to make things simple and easy for them as much as possible. Being able to keep them in the loop while handling the quick fixes, and making the bigger stuff more painless, will go a long way towards building trust, rapport and goodwill. Happy landlord, happy life!
- *Create a budget and stick to it.* Remember that your goal here is to generate cash flow from the deal. You don't own these properties – the more money you sink in, the longer it takes for you to start getting a return.

    Before committing to anything, create a realistic budget based on your market research and your assessment of the property in the viewing. Then don't spend a penny more. Knowing your numbers is vital – this means that you can immediately justify your negotiations with the hard numbers if needed (and make it clear that you are a professional at the same time!).
- *Don't cut corners.* Making good use of your time and money here is important. However, don't cheap out on things either. A rush job is

always going to be noticeable and buying the cheapest furniture generally ends up costing you more later. If you buy a cheap sofa that won't last five minutes, you will need to buy another between three to six months later.

You are trying to offer quality accommodation to your tenants or guests, and a premium service to the landlords. Making the investment to do things the right way from the start will always pay off in the long run.

Once you've got the keys, it's go time! Having a strategy for the refurb and preparing the property is vital if you want to avoid wasting time and money messing around. In Chapter 9, I offer my tried-and-tested approach to the refurb which means you get the job done and have the place ready for your first clients as quickly as possible.

The final step is to get the property filled and start generating cash flow! Chapter 10 talks about how to source tenants or guests (depending on if you're dealing with an HMO or SA), this includes marketing the properties, ensuring you have the correct paperwork in place and preparing for move-in day!

CHAPTER 9

Refurbishing the property

At this point, you have picked up the keys and the clock has started ticking. Regardless of if you have successfully negotiated a preparation period or if you are paying rent from day one, you want to get the property set up as soon as possible. The faster you can turn it around and get it ready for your clients, the sooner you can start getting the cash flow that you can invest in the next property.

On the other hand, in a five-year agreement, this refurb period might be your one and only opportunity to do work on the property. If you need to do work at a later point, it will cost you far more and take a lot more planning. The balance is to do this as quickly as possible *without* making too many compromises.

If you cut corners at this stage and fail to get the property up to scratch, it could cause issues later. If you don't do the renovation right, make sure the photos are perfect, your marketing is on-point and optimise the listing to get the most clicks, you will end up with an empty unit costing you money.

When I started out, I would be very involved at this stage – I wanted to make sure that everything was perfect. As a result, I would generally land on my feet. Even then, I would still occasionally find myself with an empty property and not know 100 per cent why.

Even after refining the process and knowing all the hacks to maximise occupancy, there is an element of trial and error to getting this right and working out a system that works for you. This is one reason why scaling your rent-to-rent business is key. If one property struggles, the income from your other properties gives you the leeway to fix things.

Have a structured process

Having to refurbish potentially multiple properties quickly and well from the start means you want to have a plan from the start. This includes having a checklist of what needs to be done and timelines of when things need to happen and how long they should take.

At the start, I would sometimes be ready for tenants and guests, only to realise the internet would be another week or that the beds were going to take five days longer than originally planned – this can get costly. Having a solid plan can save you a lot of money and stress!

This also includes having a team ready to help you – expecting to turn around an entire property by yourself is a lot for just one person. I've already talked about this in Chapter 3 – when starting out, family and friends are invaluable. Later, once you begin to get cash flow and start scaling, you want to build a team of experts to support you and cover the areas you can't.

Being able to afford the right people and creating these processes at the start is a challenge. You often don't know what or who you need until you have done it once already.

Fortunately, I have developed my own checklists and timelines to support my own processes – you now get to benefit from what I've learnt the hard way! Here, I share the following steps – if you follow them in order, you should be able to complete your refurb as painlessly as possible.

Internet

In rent-to-rent, you will be the one who is responsible for organising and paying for the internet. Typically, this will take a little bit of time to sort out – up to two weeks. This means that once the agreement has been signed (don't move before then, in case the agreement falls through and you end up locked into a two-year internet contract!) you need to order the internet as quickly as possible so it is ready to welcome your first guests or tenants from day one.

STEP 2

Utilities and meter readings

The second thing that you will be responsible for during the agreement is the utilities. Organising handing over the utilities from the previous account holder to yourself is a priority and something that you want to make sure is done right. Otherwise, you risk the headache of having a £600 utility bill from the previous tenant that you are struggling to prove is nothing to do with you.

To protect yourself from this, your first priority once you have collected the keys and taken responsibility for the property is to take meter readings. Make sure that you know where to find the water, gas, and electric meters. At the first opportunity, go to the property and take photos and recordings of all the meters.

Having time-stamped photos of the meter readings means that you can prove how much you are actually liable for in the case of any dispute or issue with the utility companies. Getting smart meters installed will save you from having to do time-consuming regular meter readings and ensure you are tracking usage so you can intervene before costs stack up. Installing smart thermostats can be a great investment as well to monitor and manage usage.

Team-building – Utilities manager

Getting the utilities wrong could be expensive. Once you begin to scale, this becomes a job in itself.

I actually employ someone whose only responsibility is to deal with the utilities and internet for my properties. Other than making sure that everything is being handled, they can also support you by paying attention to the small print that many utility or internet companies try to trick you with.

They also can ensure you are measuring use, changing direct debits accordingly, alerting tenants of overuse and even switching utility companies for cheaper options or renegotiating your deal. This can save a lot of money in the long run.

Test EVERYTHING

While negotiating the agreement, you will have agreed with the owner who would be responsible for what – including what work the landlord needs to do before handing over the property. However, it is possible that work might be needed that neither you nor the owner had been aware of. You cannot take for granted that these will be evident – it might go unnoticed until someone is actively staying in the property.

Before you begin painting or redecorating anything, go through the house testing and checking everything. The sooner you can flag things that might need fixing, the earlier you can raise them with the landlord and the more likely they will be to remedy things. This also prevents the issue later of needing to do repairs while new tenants are in the property.

A landlord's timeframes and priorities do not always line up with yours – they might be used to a more traditional letting agreement, in which the tenant would simply have to be patient and allow for works to be conducted around them while the work is finished. This can cause friction when it takes them longer to do repairs.

You might find yourself stuck between your clients and the landlord – reporting maintenance issues you can't address by yourself. During this time, you might have to offer rent reductions, refunds, or need to find alternate accommodation for your tenants. For an SA property, this is even more frustrating. Guests have a much shorter stay and you risk bad reviews damaging your reputation.

The things I recommend specifically checking are:

HEATING	PLUMBING	WHITE GOODS	ELECTRICS
Is the boiler working and in good condition?	Are there any signs of leaks on ceilings, around radiators, or particularly around showers, baths, taps and drains?	Are the dishwasher, washing machine and dryer working and connected properly?	Do all the plug sockets work?

Part three: Securing cash flow

HEATING	PLUMBING	WHITE GOODS	ELECTRICS
Do the radiators work?	Do the toilets flush effectively?	Do the fridge and freezer work? Are there any broken trays that need replacing?	Do all the switches work?
Is there hot water?			Do any light bulbs need replacing?

A priority here should be checking for leaks – water damage can cause a lot of trouble and take a long time to fix. An undetected leak might result in significant impact on the property and, therefore, your cash flow. Even something like a washing machine that is not properly connected could flood the kitchen and cause havoc the first time it's used!

I once got a property that had a lot of potential. It was a Victorian property in a breathtaking location. While it seemed a bit old and tired, I figured that some people would love it if I could play to its age and go with a Victorian theme. The bathrooms were particularly good for this theme. They were in a beautiful Victorian style and decorated with some lovely Victorian tiling.

Unfortunately, I wasn't paying complete attention when I was doing my tests in the bathroom. I ran the showers – checking they worked and could go from hot to cold – but my focus was somewhere else.

The night the first guest arrived, I got disturbed with a call complaining about one of the showers. Apparently the shower could do *either* blistering hot *or* freezing cold, it was incapable of letting someone adjust the temperature.

It turned out that the mixer cartridge needed changing. However, since the shower was so old, getting it replaced was impossible. Instead, the shower had to be replaced entirely.

This involved carefully removing all these perfect Victorian tiles I had loved so much, dismantling the original shower and running new pipes in – just to put in a new shower which would not burn someone. This was a lot of work that had to be done quickly in the first week the property was meant to be generating cash flow!

151

In the end, while the landlord kindly offered to fund the works, it still cost me around £5,000 out of pocket in cancelling the guests' booking and relocating them elsewhere. If I had actually been paying attention when I had checked the shower on the first day, I could have agreed with the landlord that it needed fixing. If that had happened, we could have pushed the preparation period to last another week or so – letting us fix this without having any pressure or costing unnecessarily.

Install key safes

This is a game-changer. Previously when setting up a property, any time someone had to get in to do work, make a quote, or deliver something, I had to be there to let them in. With a key safe, I don't need to come running every time someone needs to fit new blinds, measure for new carpets or furniture, or deliver the new washing machine.

Once you are properly in business and the property is generating cash flow, there might not be that many reasons why you might need to actually visit the property. Where possible, you want to try and automate as many of these processes as possible. Otherwise, once you start building your property portfolio, you won't end up financially free – you'll just have ended up with another day job! One of the easiest systems to automate is handing over keys or helping people get into the building. The trick is to install key safes somewhere secure and accessible. This means that if someone needs your help to get into the property, all you need to do is give them access to the safe.

TOP TIP
Change the codes between clients!

There is little point to this system if a tenant or guest still has access to the key safe after they've left. This is particularly important for SA. Get your cleaners to change the code after each stay and update your channel manager for a seamless and safe system that doesn't allow guests to return with the same code as last month!

Part three: Securing cash flow

It also means that when SA guests arrive, they are able to let themselves in without needing someone to check them in personally. For HMOs, we usually give them their keys personally, but a key safe means they can let themselves in if they get locked out somehow.

My advice is to have two exterior key safes per property: one for trades (such as workmen or cleaners) and the other for your HMO tenants or SA guests (depending on the use of the property).

Keys for trades

This key safe will be installed externally and include a master key to the property. All these codes should be stored on a property management system accessible via mobile so that if a tradesman or a member of your team needs to access the property, they can quickly have a look on their phone and enter. They can then let themselves in, do what needs to be done and replace the key when they leave.

TOP TIP
"Replace the key" is law

If a key – particularly the master key in the trades key safe – is used, it has to be replaced immediately. It is remarkably easy for a key to get put into a bag or pocket, then get forgotten. This means you could end up with an empty key safe and no clue where the key is.

This caused havoc once, when an HMO tenant lost their front door key while all their housemates were away for the weekend one Sunday evening. I had just sat down to dinner when the tenant phone went off (when it should have been switched off and locked in the office cupboard until Monday!). I still remember Lucy giving me a dramatic look, warning me that I would regret answering. She was right – she usually is!

I had hoped that it would be a simple fix – giving them the code for the master key, they let themselves back in, job done. Unfortunately, a team member of mine had walked off with it earlier that week by accident. To make things worse, they were in Paris that weekend!

I ended up having to spend the rest of the night hunting down another copy of the master key and getting it over to the tenant. At the same time, I was having to handle the tenant and convince them not to do something that would make things worse, like breaking back into the property by themselves!

Keys for HMO

Ideally, your HMO tenants won't ever need to access the key safes – the purpose here is to have a backup in case of emergencies, like the one I just described. For an HMO, I go one step further since storing all the individual room keys *and* external keys in one safe won't work. So I install an external and an internal key safe for my tenants, in addition to the external key safe for trades.

The keys in the external key safe would let them in the front door. In the larger internal key safe, they can find spare keys for their specific rooms. For security reasons, this internal key safe should only be made accessible to tenants if absolutely necessary. In most cases, the key for the front door should be enough.

Keys for SA

For SA, there are two external key safes. One is for trades, the other is for guests. When guests arrive, the self-check in process includes receiving access to the guest's key safe. This lets them get access to the keys and return them at the end of their stay without needing you or your team to be on-site.

This is particularly convenient for both you and your guests. You save yourself from needing to travel around as much. Your guests get more flexibility as to when they can check-in and out. If they don't need to wait for someone to let them in, they can arrive and check-in at whichever time suits their schedule best.

STEP 5

Marketing

Your final priority for the first few days, before you start the refurb process itself, is starting to market the property. I often find that some rent-to-renters will save this for after the refurb – however, having the property on the market early means you can start building interest and attracting clients.

In Chapter 10, I will describe marketing in more detail. One key tip will be that an essential part of successfully marketing a property is having quality photography. So, how do you market a property before you have photos of the finished product?

The bathrooms and kitchen generally don't change much during the refurb process. Remember – the refurb should only be cosmetic upgrades, changing the bathrooms or kitchen is a large project which should be left to the landlord.

This means that you can use decent photos from your phone for the early listing – updating with more professional photos later.

For the rooms, you won't have done the work yet to make the property attractive. Until the refurb is complete, you will need to use placeholder imagery to help potential tenants get a picture of what their rooms will look like.

A benefit of having a standard level of quality and style that you maintain across all of your properties is that this lets you use previous photography of other properties that give a good sense of the intended end result. With a clear disclaimer that the property is currently being newly renovated and, therefore, the photography is not the exact property, but an example of the finish you can expect, you can begin attracting tenants from the moment you have the keys.

Once you have a placeholder listing ready to go, you can post it around. In addition to this, you can share it with your network – who can then share it by word of mouth or direct any potential tenants that they find towards you.

In Chapter 10, I'll cover websites that I find particularly useful. At this stage, it's as simple as using your sample photography (which you'll replace when you have professional photographs for the "official" listing) and posting the ad live on the appropriate websites.

- For an HMO, use an online property portal such as spareroom.co.uk
- For an SA, list with an online travel agent such as Airbnb. An important point here, however, is to ensure that you have turned "instant book" off, so you can control availability and prevent someone trying to book during the refurb!

---

18 grand in six months, thanks to marketing early!

Marketing a property from the start can offer you opportunities to start generating cash flow that you might not have predicted. I once managed to start generating cash flow of three grand per month from day one thanks to this. This was a huge win, since the property would have normally required three weeks of work and an investment of somewhere between five to eight grand before I could start filling rooms.

I had just closed a deal on guaranteeing the rent for a slightly tired eight-room property that I expected to need a bit of work to refurb. The next day, a group of eight construction workers got in touch with me. They needed a place in the area in three days' time. I decided to chance it and sent them a rough video.

They agreed on the spot – apparently they couldn't find any other properties of that size – therefore, despite the standard of the property not being the best, it was perfect for them. On top of that, they offered me six grand a month to rent it. This was a brilliant deal for me – I was only guaranteeing the rent for £1,700 a month!

This meant that I could start making a profit from day one without having to invest a penny. By the time they left six months later, I'd made a total of £18,000 in net profits!

I decided to quit while I was ahead on that property and gave my notice at the four month point. When they left, I handed the keys back and invested that money into a property purchase that I'd own for myself! Rent-to-Rent 2.0 in action.

The cosmetic refurb

These steps until now are all things that can happen in the first few days. At this point, you can be confident that:

- The internet and utilities are under control and will be ready when the tenants move in.
- Everything that would require more than cosmetic work or might cause trouble has been identified, and is either being handled by you or the landlord.
- If workers need to access the property, you do not need to be there in person to let them in every time.
- You are starting to drum up interest and attract potential tenants or guests, allowing you to fill properties without any voids.

You can now start refurbishing the property itself!

Initial clean and assessment

My first step in any refurb process is to clean the entire property and everything in it from top to bottom. This prepares the property for whatever needs to be done and gives you a chance to have a close look at everything and make decisions about what needs to be addressed.

Part three: Securing cash flow

It is at this point that I will make any big decisions about what works in the property, what can be saved and what I need to get rid of. Cleaning means you need to get up close and personal with all of the fixtures, fittings and furnishings. This makes it the perfect time to start deciding "this mirror works, but the other one needs to go" or "there is no way we can save this carpet, better to get rid of it."

What is important here is to make a solid decision now and stick to it. The last thing you want is to leave something you aren't sure about, then realise that it has to go only once you have finished changing everything else. Doubt here only leads to delays – there's no point replacing five out of eight carpets one week, then realise the other three need doing a week later.

TOP TIP
Consider your tenant avatar

When making decisions about what to keep or get rid of and the work that needs to be done, think about the kind of client you are expecting to stay in the property. When you were doing your market research in Chapter 4, you will have built an "avatar" – all the decisions you need to make now should fit what this ideal client will expect to see in the property.

The eight construction workers I mentioned in Step 5 had very different expectations compared to a client looking for a luxury family rental. Since they were working 12–hour days, they didn't care if everything was perfect.

When you struggle with a decision or feel yourself becoming indecisive, try to focus on the choice which helps the property match the requirements of your ideal tenant and you will never go far wrong. This is also a great hack for ensuring you keep the budget in line with your end client's needs. No point putting luxury sofas in a property if you're going for a budget student HMO let.

Empty out everything being removed

Once you have identified everything that needs to go and following a conversation with the landlord about any existing furniture, it is time to start the "rip out" and get rid of it. Just throwing everything you don't want away can be a waste, however. While some things might be legitimately rubbish, other things might still be useful or valuable to somebody.

Often, I find that if I take photos of the old and cheap furniture I have no interest in keeping and share it on an online marketplace for £20 to £50, someone will buy it. I have cleared out houses before and ended up making £800 from furniture that I would have never expected anyone to be interested in. What I can't sell, I will often see if I can give away somehow before I commit to just throwing it away.

There are two reasons why I prefer this approach:

- It is cheaper – getting rid of rubbish gets expensive quickly. The cost of a skip adds up fast, particularly if you are operating in London or somewhere similar. The more you can pass onto others, the less you need to pay to get rid of.
- It helps those who really need it – sometimes people are in genuine need of what you are getting rid of, but can't afford it normally. Passing things on when you can means that it can get re-used, re-purposed, or recycled when it would otherwise go to waste.

Team-building – Man with a van and networks

When it comes to clearing things out of a property or moving things in, do not underestimate the value of a man with a van. Having either a friend or family member who has a suitable van, or a freelancer you can call on when needed, means you can move everything in and out quickly and efficiently when you need.

Another valuable resource is joining groups active in your area that can let you either sell or pass on what you can't sell. This might be in a network for those doing property in your area, an online community for residents letting people trade or sell things to each other, or in local upcycling groups.

Furnish and decorate

The next stage is to start furnishing and decorating. This is less about your own personal taste and more about the general quality. Remember – you aren't the one who is going to live here, what you want is to make the property attractive to tenants. The focus should be on whether the end result is something decent and nice that the tenant would be happy to rent.

> TOP TIP
> ## Design using the rule of three
>
> If you think about most big brands or successful designs, you will notice that they all have just two to three key colours and themes. It is very rare to see more than three at most. The quick explanation is that it does not overcomplicate things and ties everything together.
>
> When deciding on a style for the property, I recommend applying the rule of three. I usually pick two or three colours for the property. These colours are what I will use for the theme of the property – for example the feature walls and the main furniture.
>
> You also don't have to start designing again from scratch with every new property. If you pick a style and colour scheme and then just rinse and repeat with each new property, you never have to make these decisions again!
>
> Designing your properties like this helps create a simple and attractive look and over time means you can develop a clear and recognisable standard that all your properties are guaranteed to meet.

When it comes to sourcing furniture, there are two approaches.

When I started out, I needed to equip my properties with style and quality, but on a very limited budget. This meant getting furniture from online marketplaces or second-hand where possible. This takes a lot of legwork though and is impossible to replicate as you are buying one-off items.

Nowadays, I have systemised the process. Using mainstream stores like Ikea and Argos might cost a little bit more, but it means you can rinse and repeat every time!

I also have built relationships with local furniture companies. If ever I need to source big furniture, I can call them, order everything I need, then they deliver and set everything up for me. Thanks to the installed key safes, I don't even need to be there to let them in!

> TOP TIP
> ## Discounts and re-using furniture
>
> Look out for discount stores that get the discontinued stock from major retailers like Dunelm and Marks & Spencers. I've hunted for these companies and got high level furniture at a fraction of the price!
>
> Another tip is if you buy cheap, you buy twice. I have found investing slightly more one time means you have to replace stuff less often. It's

important to remember that buying furniture is not like painting and redecorating. You can take the furniture with you when you go. I have left deals before with entire sets of furniture that can just be moved straight into my next property without any trouble.

This builds up surprisingly quickly – I often joke that if I get out of property, I will have to open a furniture store just to have a place to keep everything!

Team-building – Your refurb squad (or power team)

I have already talked about how helpful having someone to help you move things around and source furniture are, but there are several other roles that you want to have on your team to make the refurb as painless as possible.

The handyman
Building a relationship with someone who you can trust to take care of all of the various small jobs and DIY around a property is invaluable.

Having a good handyman on your team means that you can be sure that all the jobs and repairs have been done right and to a high standard. This might involve putting in mirrors, changing toilet seats, small repairs and so on. It even could involve putting together the flatpack furniture for you.

The blinds guy
Installing the blinds is a job that is easy to overlook, but surprisingly tricky to do right. Having a specialist who knows what they are doing is a gamechanger. This means that they can come in, measure up the windows, source the blinds and install them with no hassle.

The flooring and carpet installer
Well installed flooring and carpets can make a huge difference to a refurb. As with the blinds, this can also be difficult to do right. Having someone you can call on to do a good job at this can make or break a refurb.

The painter and decorator
In terms of return on investment, nothing adds value quite like a fresh paint job. It completely transforms the space and shouldn't cost too much with the right person on hand!

These days, I actually have a full-time painter and decorator working for me. With the number of properties I'm looking after, he's always got something to do – whether it is decorating new properties or freshening up my older properties that could do with a bit of TLC.

Deep Clean

Once you have all the new furniture in place and the painting is finished, the final touch is to do one final deep clean. The aim here is to make sure that the property is in the best possible condition for the photoshoot, and for the tenants to move into.

TOP TIP
Stay on top of maintenance

The final piece of advice for the refurb is to keep on top of this. While the first few weeks are the best time to get in and do significant work, you should try to keep the property in a good condition throughout the duration of your agreement.

There are several reasons for this, but primarily, you don't want it in a condition which requires you to invest thousands to return it at the end of a five-year agreement.

For the most part, this maintenance would involve getting your painter or decorator to freshen up the paint and making sure that any minor repairs are done. The best time for this would be in the few days between tenancies or bookings.

Even the longest HMO tenant is most likely to only stay for 18 months. When they move out, this is a good opportunity to go in and touch up the room.

STEP 7
The photoshoot

When you started the refurb, you will have made a "placeholder" listing for the property. This might have included placeholder images or photos taken from your smartphone. This should not be what you use for the final listing – you need to get professional photos of the refurbished property.

Too often, I see rookies relying on images they took themselves on their smartphones. They never get around to updating the listing with more professional photos. Two months later, they are wondering why they aren't getting any bookings!

Getting a professional to take photos before any clients move in is a fantastic investment. At this point, the property is as good as it is ever going to look – even the best tenant is going to cause wear and tear to the property. On top of this, good photos can be used for everything from marketing the property to providing examples to sceptical landlords of the quality they can expect from you.

Finding an expert photographer

Taking photos of a property is a very specific skill set and requires professional equipment – cameras with wide lenses are vital for example, since they help create an impression of size and space in the room. If you are part of a network, I recommend asking the people you know in property, to put you in touch with a good photographer.

Otherwise, you have to get creative. A helpful tip is to look around local letting agents – either in person or online – to find ones who have particularly good photography. You can then ask them to put you in touch with the person who took them.

Managing the photoshoot

Before the photoshoot itself, there are two things to consider: lighting and setting the scene.

The lighting in the photos needs to be as natural as possible – artificial lighting is typically far less flattering. This means that you want to take photos during the day. Since the photoshoot should take a couple of hours – you want as many photos as possible taken well – be careful of booking the photographer too late in the afternoon.

It is also a good idea to include touches that dress the property and make it look more attractive and welcoming. This could include plants and flowers or nice touches like extra throws or cushions. Generally, these won't all be things that you want to leave in the property afterwards, however. My recommendation is to have a supply of props and decorations you keep safe in storage, ready for photoshoots.

It can be easy to try to cut corners and take the photos in as short a time as possible. Don't rush this process or you risk mistakes or something embarrassing slipping through. You should make sure that all wires and cables are tucked out of sight, the beds are made (I recommend ironed bedding if possible) and any labels on cushions or throws are not visible.

You also want to avoid something being accidentally included in the photo. This might include bags or jackets on furniture, or even something like a Starbucks cup in the middle of a table!

The photos themselves should all be landscape – this allows them to fill the screen properly without any distracting white lines when viewed online. You also want to have as many taken as possible. This allows you to really show off even the fine details of the property. I find that the algorithm tends to work in your favour if your listing has around 25 or more photos of the property.

I generally prefer to focus on interior photos, however, it never hurts to include one or two exterior photos. This is particularly true if the property has some kind of attractive exterior feature such as a nice garden or a particularly impressive view.

Another touch that I am starting to include in all of my listings is a 3D tour of the property. This allows for a viewing experience without needing the client to visit the property in person. It also gives them a chance to see the property in its best light, before any wear or tear from use. If the photographer has the ability to create a 3D tour, this is well-worth including.

The final thing you can do here is to create a video of the property. The benefit of this is for your portfolio. This allows you to share videos of your properties on social media and your website. Landlords can get a sense of the services you offer. Clients, whether HMO tenant or SA guest, can get a sense of the quality of your properties in general – potentially leading to a guest who enjoyed their stay in one property coming to you specifically in the future.

Now you have the professional photos and videos, it's time to add them to the listing you made earlier. Once that's done, you're live and ready to go! It's time to start welcoming clients and generating cash flow!

YOU SHOULD HAVE	<ul><li>All internet and utilities scheduled and organised</li><li>Photos of the meters on the day you took charge of the property</li><li>Confirmation that everything in the property works and is in good condition</li><li>Key safes installed for the tenants/guests and for any tradesmen</li><li>Placeholder marketing for the property</li><li>The cosmetic refurb completed</li><li>Professionally-taken photographs for marketing the property and building your own portfolio</li></ul>

CHAPTER 10

The Pay-Off – Securing Cash Flow

So, now the refurb is done, you need to start generating your cash flow by finding clients to fill the property. If you can't fill your properties, then you aren't going to generate the income which allows you to guarantee the rent, generate the cash flow you hoped for, and ultimately continue to scale to your financial goals.

TOP TIP
Be patient

It may take time to build momentum when it comes to filling properties – especially in the early days. While you do need to make sure you're stepping it up at this point, don't panic if the property doesn't fill instantly.

This is the key reason why I always advise negotiating that the agreement lasts between three to five years. The length of the agreement allows you plenty of time to get a return on investment. The key is to stay calm and trust the process – if you have done everything up to this point correctly, you'll have nothing to worry about.

If it takes a while to find the right tenants for an HMO, or perhaps the SA bookings start off slowly for a few weeks, it's a tiny per cent of the total term. While you don't want to lose money by wasting time, taking the time to get things right, find the right clients, and get your systems up to speed always pays off in the long run.

One bad HMO tenant could cost you thousands in disruptions and court costs. A bad experience for SA guests could cause costs and damages; while also leading to poor reviews to deal with that may result in long-term occupancy issues.

During the refurb, one of your first priorities is to start placeholder marketing in order to start building interest and sourcing tenant leads. If you are lucky, this might already be bearing fruit. This might look different depending on if you are marketing the property as an HMO or as SA.

Filling an HMO

Marketing

For HMO, you might be sourcing early leads through word-of-mouth, curious locals, or your initial marketing. Don't be afraid to let these early, eager leads view the property while doing the refurb. In fact, I often find that tenants will get excited by seeing the property while work is on-going. It lets them start to buy into your finished vision and shows them that they are guaranteed to get a freshly renovated and high quality place to live.

When it comes to marketing the property itself, the internet is an invaluable resource. The main websites I would recommend might already look familiar from your market research:

- Spareroom.co.uk – this is one of the biggest house share websites in the UK. As a landlord, this is a fantastic resource to find tenants looking to rent just a room.
- Openrent.co.uk – OpenRent is a fantastic website that magnifies your marketing reach while costing next to nothing. It allows you to have a presence on some of the more well-known online property portals – getting lots of eyeballs on your properties – for a fraction of the cost. At the time of writing, £30 for three months of OpenRent vs £700–800 per month to get on Rightmove (along with a lot of hoops to jump through!).
- Facebook – what better place to market your properties than on the biggest social media platform with over three billion people!

The last time you were on these websites, you were looking to source properties. This time, you're on the other side of the interaction (you may even find yourself getting offers from aspiring rent-to-renters from this point!).

At this point, you need to create an account and ad for your property – if you haven't already. Once you have done that, you can upload your professional photos of the property, make sure you have an available listing for each room, and write a description to make the listing attractive to your target tenant.

Part three: Securing cash flow

Qualifying potential tenants
Once the marketing starts bringing in leads, you want to make sure that you are working smart and not wasting your time on unsuitable tenants. At the start, I would invest hours coming over to the property to show prospective tenants around and building rapport – only to discover they couldn't move in for five months or were just window-shopping to get a feel for the area!

I've developed a two-stage process that can help you work out if a lead might be a suitable tenant. This allows you to weed out time wasters or anyone who might become a headache down the line.

Step one is to send anyone responding to your ads a questionnaire – either as a webform or something they need to fill out and either text or email back to you. The information you want to collect is:

- Name
- Contact details (telephone number and email address)
- Employment status (or are you a student?)
- Annual salary
- When do you want to move in?
- Are you a smoker?
- Is there anything you really want to have in a housemate?
- Is there anything you really *don't* want to have in a housemate?

Once they have filled out the questionnaire, check whether they seem to be a decent prospect. If they are a good match, then it is time to move onto step two and have a quick phone call with them.

At this point, your goal is to get a sense of who they are and how easy they might be to live with, and be in communication with. If they come across as somebody who you feel is in line with the target tenant and someone you could get along with, then you may have found yourself a great tenant – for you and (more importantly) any other tenants they will be living with.

TOP TIP
Avoiding discrimination

As a landlord, it is important to avoid discriminating against a potential tenant regarding what are called "protected characteristics". According to the Equality Act 2010, these include:

1. Age
2. Disability
3. Gender reassignment
4. Marriage or civil partnership
5. Pregnancy and maternity
6. Race (including: skin colour, nationality, ethnic or national origins)
7. Religion or belief
8. Sex
9. Sexual orientation

Viewings

Ideally, you want to fill a property in one go, rather than spreading viewings out over several days. This means that the best way to do viewings is as a block of time for somewhere between five to ten leads at once. Having everyone there together serves several purposes:

- It creates a sense of scarcity and urgency, this helps you secure tenants sooner and more effectively.
- It provides the tenants a chance to meet the people they are going to be living with. If they hit it off with each other, they will be more interested in renting together – or be more likely to apply if they hear that someone else they liked has reserved a room already.

As an example, you would start at midday one Saturday afternoon, then show each tenant the property over 15-minute intervals. Over this time, your goal is to pay attention to their motivators and any objections they might have to the property.

Ideally, you want to encourage them to commit as quickly as possible. Once a tenant has expressed interest, I recommend asking them to pay a small holding rent of £150 to hold the room for them while the application process is completed.

It is important to note that this holding rent is not a reservation fee. Instead, this is a partial advance payment on their first month of rent – having paid an advance helps solidify the tenant's commitment to the room. If either you or the tenant need to pull out, this money must be refunded.

Finalising the paperwork

When qualifying the tenant originally, you will have asked them about any issues which might disqualify them from renting. At this point, you need to check these qualifying details more officially – if you have done things right so far, there shouldn't be any huge surprises!

I recommend checking for the following:

- Proof of their right to rent in the UK – check www.gov.uk/prove-right-to-rent for examples of eligible documents.
- Proof of employment if they are working
  - Payslips
  - Work contract or job offer if the job is brand new
- Proof of entry to their university if they are a student – either their Student ID or proof of entry to university if they are a new student
- References
- Affordability checks for the tenant or their guarantor if they do not have earnings (either a parent or next-of-kin)
- Credit checks

Once they have passed the official application process, then you send them the tenancy agreement. After they have signed this, then you are ready for them to move in officially.

Your next step is to do an official inventory of the property before they move in. In addition to this, if you are taking a deposit, you have to store the money in a secure deposit protection scheme.

TOP TIP
Get the legalities right from the start

It is vital that you make sure that your tenants have been served the correct legal documents to make the contract binding. Both you and the tenant need to have signed them and everyone involved needs their own copies.

If the tenant is not served the correct documents by the time they have moved in, you are potentially opening yourself up to a world of risk. Without having followed the correct legal process, you will find things almost impossible if you need to evict them later.

These include:

1. An Energy Performance Certificate
2. Deposit prescribed information
3. A current gas safety certificate
4. A copy of the property licence
5. How to Rent Guide (found at "www.gov.uk/government/publications/how-to-rent")

Deposits

Taking a deposit has several legal requirements you need to follow, but offers you protection from damages at the end of the tenant's contract. A deposit needs to be put in a deposit protection scheme. Failing to protect a deposit you have been paid potentially means being ordered to pay up to three times the deposit back to the tenant – best avoided!

Once a tenancy ends, if the tenant has done deliberate damage to the property, you can request to claim money from the protected deposit. This is when a detailed inventory becomes important, as it allows you to provide the detailed and precise evidence as to what the damages were that the third party will demand as proof.

Marketing SA

Marketing

There are hundreds of Online Travel Agents (OTA) to choose from when marketing a SA property, but the most popular websites I recommend starting with are:

- Airbnb
- Booking.com
- Vrbo
- Tripadvisor
- Google Business

You will notice that most of these websites are what are called "Online Travel Agents" (OTAs) rather than direct booking websites. While OTAs are more expensive – they charge a commission anywhere between 3 and 18 per cent – they are also the easiest way to get eyes on your property quickly. Eventually we are going to look towards taking as many direct bookings as possible via your own direct booking website, but at the beginning the easier way to get bookings is by using OTAs.

While building a presence on direct booking websites is valuable, you can't escape the fact that 99 out of 100 of your guests are going to start looking on Google. This means you want to develop an optimised presence over as many of the available platforms as possible.

If you have started this marketing process during the refurb, you might even have already received bookings for your new property listing. Since you can set the availability on your booking websites, the only immediate change you need to make when finalising the refurb is updating your listing with your new professionally-taken photos and removing the disclaimer that you had attached to the previous placeholder images.

Generally, the turnaround time for SA is much shorter than for HMOs. It is entirely possible to get last-minute bookings from day one. However, you will still have gaps in SA, so your aim is to have your property booked for at least 50 per cent of the time in order to start breaking even.

From there, you can begin to scale occupancy rates to start generating more cash flow and profit. As you start generating more and more positive reviews, you can start to raise the nightly rate for your unit – reducing some of the pressure to maintain high occupancy all of the time. You may also want to look into smart pricing that assess local prices and suggest a price which affords you the maximum rates while still remaining competitive.

Qualifying guests

Unlike an HMO, your SA guests will need to pay the full cost of their stay before arrival. Once they have checked in, the money will be released to your allocated bank account through the platform. In some instances, you can opt to take payment through your online payment merchant account instead.

Although you are guaranteed your income, you still need to ensure you qualify your guests to avoid any in-stay issues such as damage to the property, illegal activity, or other unforeseen circumstances. The main things I consider are:

- Taking copies of photo ID – It is essential to obtain the primary guest's ID to verify the booking. This is also important if you are required to provide evidence of who was staying at the property.

- Ensure guests sign your terms and conditions – Whether a guest books directly with you or via an OTA, it is essential your guest signs your terms and conditions so that if damage is caused you have written authority to deduct the money from their card.
- Pre-authorise their damage deposit – Like any hotel you want to pre-authorise a damage deposit so that in the event any damage is caused, you can automatically charge their card as per your terms and conditions.

PRO-TIP
Trust your instincts

As effective as the above methods are, it is essential to follow your gut. If a guest seems suspicious, it may be worth getting them on the phone and finding out a little bit more about the purpose of their stay.

Another great way to assess a guest on OTAs is to check when their account was created and any past reviews.

Although some OTAs can penalise hosts for cancellations, if in doubt, I always cancel any bookings that don't feel right. I learned this the hard way though allowing guests I had a bad feeling about to stay in my property who then caused serious damage. Honestly, it's not worth the risk.

Checking in

You want to make sure that the check-in process itself is as automated as possible. This involves setting up the systems to ensure the guest has all the information they need to easily find, access and enjoy their stay at your property.

You want to avoid needing to attend the property to check in every guest – particularly since guests will often arrive at unpredictable times.

What I do is share a link with all the relevant information with guests before they check in. This contains guide videos that show them around the property, helps them access the key safe, and demonstrates how to use various things around the property. These videos are things that could be produced during the professional photoshoot at the end of the refurb.

> TOP TIP
> ## Have a house manual for guests
>
> It is a good idea to have a physical house manual in the property for guests' stays. This will save you lots of back and forth explaining how to use a shower, un-trip the power or share the password to the WiFi.

The power of positive reviews

With SA, reviews are king! So, just because the guests have checked in and you have secured your first income does not mean your work stops. Do everything you can to make their stay great and go the extra mile. Reviews will be the cornerstone of your business and will have a massive impact on your listings long term success.

At this point, all that is left to do is to start hunting down the next property. From here, you can keep scaling until you've met the goals you set for yourself all the way back in Chapter 2!

Good luck!

YOU SHOULD HAVE	• The property marketed and set up with the professional pictures taken in Chapter 9 • A non-discriminatory method for qualifying and vetting tenants • A solid agreement making sure you are legally covered • A system for protecting deposits from tenants • A system for qualifying guests • A check-in system that is as automated as possible

Conclusion

Rent-to-Rent 2.0 – The future

Of all the property strategies I've encountered and tried, none have ever measured up to the power of rent-to-rent. Its potential for scalability and growth, while providing a source of cash flow that can replace your work income without taking over your life, can't be ignored.

The challenge that rent-to-rent beginners face isn't the potential of the strategy, it's that learning how to do it takes a lot of trial and error. So many people, myself included, find themselves buried under a barrage of "no"s and rejection when they are trying to get started.

With Rent-to-Rent 2.0, it's time for that to change.

Through years of hard work and experimenting, I have discovered the secrets and tricks that any beginner deserves to know from the beginning. After having tried and tested them myself, I passed them on as a mentor and coach – helping thousands of people get started and find success for themselves. Through writing this book, I am sharing these with the world and making sure that anyone can access what I wish I had known when I started.

If you have followed my advice, you can now start your own Rent-to-Rent 2.0 business, confident that you can overcome all of the hurdles between you and securing cash flow from your first deals.

PRIORITY ONE
Preparation

The first priority is ensuring that you are completely prepared before you even step foot into a property. The core of Rent-to-Rent 2.0 is being able to position yourself as a professional property expert. Achieving this requires you to have done your homework first.

You need to have focused and achievable goals and targets that allow you to build a set of measurable goals and targets for yourself, and your new business. The key to this is knowing what your available assets are and being clear on what you want to achieve.

Once you are clear on where you are going, you need to establish a credible business presence that is compliant with all the necessary regulations, protects your personal assets, and establishes you are a professional that landlords can trust with their properties. Amazingly, this is something that almost every course seems to skip, leaving beginners to work it out for themselves. My simple-to-follow framework walks you through each step, allowing you to get this right the first time.

The final piece of preparation to do is market research to build a realistic idea of what you are looking for in your area and what will work best for you as an SA or HMO. My top-ten property green flags mean that you can pinpoint exactly what type of properties you need to meet your goals, as well as the client profile and strategy that will work best.

ANNE AND JEFF
Replaced their work income with £5,000 in passive income, in just 12 months!

Anne and Jeff were both tired of the stresses of their nine-to-fives and wanted to create more freedom and certainty in their lives. They found their first deal through a letting agent on Gumtree – a fantastic 6-bed HMO that had just finished being fully refurbished. The only thing needed from them was to add in soft furnishings and any final touches, before finding tenants.

It turned out, however, that there were several agents in the mix who had not told the landlord exactly what Anne and Jeff were offering. For a heart-wrenching moment, it looked like the deal was going to fall through.

The duo had already found two potential tenants, but since the keys had been taken back and there was no contract, they couldn't move forward. So they went directly to the landlord to work things out.

It soon became clear that the landlord had not been told about any of the benefits Anne and Jeff was offering them. In addition to a guaranteed rent payment of £2,000 every month, they would handle all of the stress of running the property for them: no management fees, no need to worry about managing bills or finding tenants.

The landlord accepted on the spot.

Anne and Jeff quickly got to work. From their first property alone, they are making £900 positive cash flow a month, and they haven't stopped there! In their first 12 months, they managed to close five other properties as well. From all six properties combined, they were making a total of £5,000 every month. Today, they have managed to double this!

Conclusion

This passive income is more than enough to live off, and replace their previous work income. This means they have both had the freedom to quit their old jobs, and reclaim their time and energy - spending more time with their family and enjoying the important things in life.

Sourcing the leads

Once you are set up, it's time to get stuck in. At this stage, you've got to source leads and secure viewings. Not every landlord or agent is going to be the perfect fit, so it's vital that you know what you are doing as you assess them and the property while building the rapport and understanding that will let you position your offer precisely and build an agreement that benefits everyone.

Sourcing your first deals particularly can be intimidating. I've shared with you my favourite strategies for getting in touch with agents or landlords and how to secure the all-important viewing.

A common trap for the inexperienced is to charge in without paying attention to what the landlord or agents actually wants from rent-to-rent. Without knowing what motivates or concerns them, your offer simply won't land. I've shared the most common motivations and objections I come across - allowing you to know what you need to look for.

It is also important to make sure that the property itself is suitable. I've shared my advice on what you need to look for during the viewing process to assess the property and calculate if it represents a good investment.

Rent-to-rent is not a standard arrangement and it can't be done with a landlord or agent's standard agreements. If the prospect and property are suitable, then you need to make the offer, negotiate terms and use the correct agreement to ensure it is a win-win for everyone. I have broken this down into five simple steps that ensure that you stay perfectly covered without anything getting missed out or overwhelming the other party.

KEISHA & NATHANIEL
The perfect location

Keisha & Nathaniel's first rent-to-rent deal is perfect for a student HMO client avatar. Not only is it right in Leicester City Centre, but it is just around the corner from De Montfort University. It even backs onto the student hall. Both this and its good condition meant the property stood out to them from the moment they first saw it.

Another benefit for the duo is they get to deal directly with the laidback landlord, whose main motivator, since they had no mortgage, is just to get a guaranteed monthly rent with no further hassle. Thanks to such a flexible landlord, this opens the opportunity for them to operate serviced accommodation during the summer months to visitors and tourists and an HMO for students during the rest of the year.

The refurb was similarly simple – a £3,000 cosmetic refurb and £3,000 spent on furnishings. As the furnishings represent company assets, they simply needed to make £4,500 to break even on the investment. Thanks to a monthly cash flow of £650 per month after all rent and bills had been paid, this means they broke even in just seven months.

Two years later they have earnt just shy of £25k.

P.S. They now have 12 similar properties under their belt. Nathaniel has quit his day job.

Cash flow

The final challenge of rent-to-rent is making sure the refurb goes perfectly and you manage to secure the cash flow that lets you scale to the next deal. Getting either wrong could go very badly, so you need to approach these with a structured framework, rather than working it out as you go.

In the refurb, cutting corners and skipping steps only leads to delays and issues later on. I have broken the refurb process down into a seven-step process that works for any property. This means that you can ensure that every deal you take on can be guaranteed to be refurbished to the same high-quality, reinforcing your reputation.

Securing cash flow means just one thing – ensuring that your new HMO or SA is filled and you are earning the money you need from the property. I've

Conclusion

talked you through the process of securing both tenants and guests – depending on your chosen approach – allowing you to start making cash flow from day one!

SAM AND OLI
Breaking even in under 4 months

As ex-soldiers, Sam and Oli were uncertain about their future and needed a financial plan for the next chapter of their lives. Rent-to-Rent 2.0 was an exciting solution.

Now, normally I don't recommend going for flats but this one was different. For one thing, it's not just within the five mile range of home I recommend, Oli lives just two minutes down the road! This means that Oli knew for a fact the area would be perfect - affluent and cosy with a safe feel, but still just 30 minutes away from Central London.

They were able to put an offer in immediately after viewing the property and things moved fast from there. With minimal refurb work needed, they managed to get the keys on Thursday and have their first booking ready to go by Sunday! It's been fully booked pretty much constantly ever since.

Between the deposit and furnishing the property, it cost Sam and Oli just £5,500 to set up. With a monthly cash flow of around £1,300 to £1,500, this meant that they broke even in under four months - exactly what you want from a rent-to-rent deal. From that point on, any and all cash flow was a brilliant opportunity to invest in their next deal! 12 months later and the guys are hitting over £5000 a month cash flow and well on their way to creating the financial stability they were looking for.

What next?

At this point, your first property is up and running, congratulations! The next step is to rinse and repeat, using the cash flow from your first deal to start scaling your Rent-to-Rent 2.0 business into a property empire. Once you build up enough cash flow, you can start investing this into property you *do* own for long term legacy wealth. Once you have replaced your income through assets you own, then you've made it.

This isn't a job you have to do alone. If you try to manage everything by yourself, you'll soon get to the point where you find yourself spending every second working. Throughout this book, I have pointed out opportunities for building a team to help and support you. Using this, you can start to build and systemise the whole process of rent-to-rent, both sourcing deals and managing the properties, allowing you to reclaim your time and focus on what is really important.

If you get all this right you will eventually be able to remove yourself from the business, having a team to run it with you overseeing things from your mobile phone anywhere in the world. Goals.

Over the last five years, rent-to-rent has utterly changed my life. I started out at the bottom with very little and I did not have a clue what I was doing in property. Fast forward to today and it's hard to believe I have multiple 7-figure property businesses, and I finally have the financial independence to live freely and enjoy life. Rent-to-Rent 2.0 is the king of cash flow. This stuff works.

It is not easy though. It is hard and it is challenging. The key is making a choice, getting up off the sofa, and getting started. You need to put in the time and effort and of course get educated so you know what you are doing, but trust me: if I can do it, you can too

By reading this book, you've made that first step. Now you just have to follow through.

One last thing, whatever you do, don't wait 25 years. Start today.

Good luck.

Simon Smith

About the Author

Born and bred in Derby, Simon is a successful property investor specialising in Rent-to-Rent 2.0, HMO, Serviced Accommodation and BRRRR, and has established himself internationally as the go-to source of knowledge on Rent-to-Rent. Previously working full-time in the music industry, Simon had realised that his income was not reliable – no matter how successful he became, it was too feast-or-famine to provide any stability for Simon and his family.

Discovering the world of property investment gave Simon the key he was looking for. From a standing start and with no previous experience in property, Simon has managed to transform his initial investment of £3,000 to build a 7-figure property business generating over £1,000,000 annual revenue And the craziest thing about it is this is all from property he does not own!

But he hasn't stopped there. Simon's innovative and creative business model allows him to rapidly scale a portfolio of purchased properties he does own, which is now also worth over £3,000,000 – fully funded through his Rent-to-Rent 2.0 cashflow. After transforming his life through property, Simon has found a passion for helping others succeed.

Simon knows all about the strengths – and weaknesses – of traditional rent-to-rent, and found a better way to run a rent-to-rent business, which he calls Rent-to-Rent 2.0. This is a cutting edge approach that allows you to run a flexible and scalable property business that guarantees cash flow and passive income

Find out more about Simon at simonsmithonline.com.

Scan the QR code

Printed in Great Britain
by Amazon